The Real Miracle

A GUIDE TO YOUR INNER BEING

BARBARA & JIMMIE LEWIS

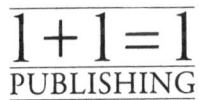

The Real Miracle
Copyright © 2002
By
Barbara & Jimmie Lewis

The Real Miracle:
A Guide to Your Inner Being
Copyright © 2015
By
Jimmie Lewis

All rights reserved.

1+1=1 Publishing
1344 Jones Street
Sonoma, CA 95476
1plus1publishing@gmail.com

Printed in the United States of America

First Edition: April 2002

Second Edition: April 2015

10 9 8 7 6 5 4 3 2 1

ISBN: 978-0-9914629-3-3

Dedication

*The Real Miracle is dedicated to
the miracle that Barbara Lewis
really was, and is, and to the voice
in which it is written, which is hers.*

*Barbara Ann Kenney Lewis
May 23, 1953 – August 31, 2010*

Acknowledgements

*To Michael and Phyllis Lewis Hyland
for their belief in me.*

*To Phyllis Lewis Hyland
for her untiring efforts
on my behalf.*

Contents

	Prologue	1
	Introduction	5
Chapter 1:	Unchangeable Creation	11
Chapter 2:	Heaven on Earth	29
Chapter 3:	Spiritual Eyes	49
Chapter 4:	Innocent and Blameless	61
Chapter 5:	The Heart of Truth	79
Chapter 6:	Our True Nature	103
Chapter 7:	An Instant of Truth	121
Chapter 8:	The Miracle	145
Chapter 9:	A Powerful Way of Life	161
Chapter 10:	The Real Miracle	175

Prologue

*Yet what is true in God's creation cannot enter here
until it is reflected in some form the world can understand.*
—A Course in Miracles, Lesson 138

This book is a reflection of the form that we could understand, in a very practical and human way, the miracle of who we really are.

Barbara was told in meditation to write this book. She didn't want to because she was working full-time in a very demanding job and she had spent a lot of time and energy on our first book, *The Energy of Life,* under the same circumstances.

Her guide throughout this book is a well-known and revered Diety and he told her he could keep her up all night until she agreed to write the book. Barbara knew the book was for her own learning, and mine, just as *The Energy of Life* was. She came downstairs after her meditation and told me what had happened and that she had agreed to write the new book, she just didn't know the name of it yet.

So we began our collaboration, Barbara and I, and with guidance from what we received in meditation.

In updating *The Real Miracle*, I have seen that the circumstances we have described herein are precisely what Barbara and I needed to go through in order to release ourselves from the fear that was covering up our Divinity.

If you are now reading *The Real Miracle*, there is a reason this book is in your hands and I assure you that you will be in good hands throughout your experience of reading the book.

I recommend that you read *The Real Miracle* the way I read all inspirational books, by pausing frequently to reflect on the meaning symbolized by its words. If you will integrate *The Real Miracle*, one truth at a time, into your consciousness I believe you will have an experience of knowing something about yourself either for the first time or at a level deeper than ever before.

Thank you for joining Barbara and I through *The Real Miracle*. And may you find, and experience, the real miracle of you.

Introduction

We have to be utterly broken before we can realize that it is impossible to better the truth. It is the truth we deny which so tenderly and forgivingly picks up the fragments and puts them together again.
—Laurens Van der Post

There are things that happen on this journey we call life. Some of these things are such intense experiences that they cause us to question our deepest spiritual roots and beliefs. Usually, the kind of things that cause this kind of questioning are not our happiest and most pleasant of moments, like getting a promotion or the birth of a child. The ones that cause us to question life, God, and ourselves are the ones we tend to refer to as an incident, accident, failure, disaster or crisis. Divorce, rape, betrayal, bankruptcy, death of a parent, death of a child, diagnosis of a fatal illness and getting fired from a job are all examples of the kinds of experiences that sometimes cause us to question very deeply the meaning of life.

All of the above examples are situations that one or both of us have personally experienced in this lifetime and each experience caused us to question what we really believed at our deepest levels. But nothing threw us quite so much as our recent financial crisis. Even the death of our triplets in 1994, as painful as that was, didn't cause as much spiritual upheaval as having our financial security stripped away.

We'd like to give you a little background. We have been together now for 14 years. During those years we have greatly prospered. Both of us ended up with corporate jobs with 6 figure salaries. We loved our financial lifestyle, yet we both yearned for a different situation because our jobs wanted more of our time than we really wanted to give them.

What we wanted most of all was to be able to spend more time together and working in corporate America seemed to be the antithesis of that. In corporate America we felt as though our companies controlled how we spent the majority of our time. In other words, our companies could significantly alter any plans that we made and the time we spent together was what was left over after our companies took the largest portion. Robert Heilbroner is quoted as saying, "Time is the new poverty." We began to feel that way in corporate America. We had money but no time.

We meditated and prayed for a new vehicle for earning money to manifest in our lives. Right on cue a miraculous new vehicle for earning income evolved. Jimmie took a course on stock market strategies and started doing so well that it became obvious to us that he should quit his job. A year later, and several more courses behind us, we were doing so well that Barbara also was able to quit her job.

We were earning more in the stock market than the two of us earned together working in corporate America and what's more, we actually enjoyed the work. However, the very month that Barbara's last paycheck arrived, our financial condition changed. We made a series of errors in the stock market and within two months we lost three fourths of our total net worth. What seemed to be worse was that all of our money was tied up in stocks that had lost most of their value and so we had no way of producing any more income.

On top of that, our accountant called to inform us that we owed a large sum for last year's taxes and we still had to pay estimated taxes for the money we had earned "on paper" for the quarter we had just finished. The taxes wiped out all of our savings and we even had to borrow money from our broker to pay the rest of them. In short, we found ourselves in the deepest financial crisis either one of us had ever faced. This was the first time that our very security in this world had been threatened. We had no jobs and the vehicle we counted on for income was no longer valid.

This book is a catalog of the questioning we went through and the answers we were given. We started out searching for the secrets of manifesting prosperity in our lives and ended up with more miracles than we ever imagined. We learned a lot about the secrets of manifesting what you want in this life but the real miracle was the change that took place within our belief system.

We always thought we knew who we were. We were great at lip service to the idea that we were an expression of God. But when the financial crisis hit, we realized how shaky that belief really was. We had no idea who we really were. Our fears so engulfed us that our prior beliefs were shaken to the core. It is this core that we finally discovered. This book is about that discovery. We were looking for a miracle. We thought the miracle was going to be a miraculous turn-around in our financial situation, but it turned out that we were the real miracle. Of course, the financial situation turned around as well but that was just a result of the real miracle of us discovering who we really were.

Whether you use the pain of our examples, or the pain of your own examples, or both, as stimulus to open your mind to a whole new way of seeing yourself and the world, we hope that this book will help you, too, to discover the real miracle in you.

Wealth is not only what you have but it is also what you are.
—Sterling W. Still

Chapter 1

Unchangeable Creation

*Whatever authority I may have
rests solely on knowing how little I know.*
—Socrates

When our very security in this world seemed threatened we went through the normal fears and thoughts like "What is going to happen to us? Will we lose our house? How long will it take before we completely run out of money? What will our family and friends think?" Our minds and emotions would vacillate between panic and self-judgment. The things we thought we knew all of a sudden became very fuzzy. We remembered the old Chinese proverb, "To know and not to do is not to know." We realized that we didn't really know.

We thought for years that we grasped the concept that all humans are actually expressions of God's energy. But God certainly didn't seem present in this situation. And He certainly didn't seem connected to us. Yet we knew in our hearts that He must be. But if He really was present and connected, then why were we running around like panicked rats in a financial cage?

We also thought we believed unequivocally that we were responsible for the creation of everything in our lives. How, then, we began to question, could we have created this huge financial mess? There was a big part in each of us that denied that we had any part in creating any of it.

We remembered that there had been many things in our lives before that we had easily taken responsibility for creating. Some of those weren't very pleasant. What was different about this one? We realized that the bigger the trouble or problem, the more we had a tendency to deny any responsibility for creating it. Very similar to a child with his/her parents, the more trouble the child thinks he/she is in, the more there is a tendency for the child to lie his/her way out of the trouble. We discovered the similarity between our childhood lies and our adult denials was that both behaviors just got us in deeper trouble.

In the beginning we realized that we really knew very little and the kinds of questions we started asking got very basic. "Who am I? What am I? Where did I come from? Is this a game? Did anybody tell God that I'm in trouble over here? Did He hear? Is He going to do something about it? Did He forget about me? Did He know me in the first place? Does He love me?"

Then our minds would race and try to figure out a rational way out of the experience. Maybe we could do this or maybe we could do that. The more we thought about it the greater the fear got until, exhausted by our own efforts to leave this spiritual tarpaper, we surrendered to the experience and our learning began.

We weren't able to trade stocks while our money was tied up so we decided that we would tackle this situation from a spiritual vantage point. To us, all problems are spiritual problems. They just come disguised as financial, relationship, work and health problems.

We began to spend our days reading inspirational materials and meditating. We read all kinds of inspirational materials from traditional Christian authors to A Course in Miracles to philosophies of Far Eastern masters. Most days, we would stay in meditation all day long and spend dinnertime sharing with each other what we had learned.

Sometimes, we would meditate and read for about four hours and then spend some time trying to figure out the mistakes we had made in the stock market so we wouldn't make the same mistakes again. A part of us still thought that we had just made some bad decisions and that if we could instead make good decisions we would never create a financial mess like this again.

It didn't take us long to realize that the answer didn't lie in making better trading decisions. The answer was much deeper than that. It soon became clear to us that all of our decisions were really based on our beliefs in who we are, who God is, and what kind of world we live in.

We finally came to understand that the real power was in getting a true perspective of our identity and God's. The way we view ourselves, the way we view God and the way we view the world affects not only our decisions but it also literally affects everything in our lives. So we started our spiritual questioning/meditation sessions with very basic questions about God and ourselves.

We took one question at a time with us into meditation and we recorded the answers that we were given. We started with our concept of who God is because without God's identity straight, we knew our concept of who we are would be warped.

Who is God and what is He like?

God is indescribable. Putting God into words limits Him and He is truly unlimited. But to answer the question words must be used. Just know that however great and powerful the word, God is more. God is powerful. He can achieve all things. God is loving. He can be no other way. It would be against His nature for God is love.

God is whole. He cannot be divided or be separate from Himself. God is omnipresent. He is everywhere and there is nowhere that He is not. God is lavishly abundant. He needs nothing and has everything. God is limitless. He has no beginning and no end. He is everywhere and is everything. God knows everything. There is nothing that is not known to Him. God is unchangeable. Neither His nature, nor His mind, can be changed. God is creative. He cannot not create. God is eternal. He lives in infinity.

Who are we?

We are direct expressions of God's energy.
We are the result of God enjoying
the thought of Himself as us.

God extended His spirit outward into all that is and that creation is what we are.

All of creation, with all of its various forms, has its genesis and its underlying essence as the spirit of God. And we use the creative energy of spirit that we are to make up the world we see.

We are therefore made of, and as, the creative energy of God because there was nothing for man to be created out of except God.

In that moment of our creation, God existed as formless spirit. The spirit we call God was everything and there was nothing He was not. He was everywhere and there was nowhere He was not.

How then, could He have created anything that was not of Himself? That would have been, and is, a metaphysical impossibility.

In the moment of creation, our creation, nothing existed except for the essence, or spirit, of God. And the creative manifestation of spirit is the energy of God.

If we as humans can accept the concept of being created from God's energy, it still seems hard for us to accept that in that moment we were given the fullness of everything God was and had.

We tend to believe that we are only part of God. We see parts of God within ourselves and others. We witness power, love, creativity and abundance within ourselves and others. But what we don't realize is that everything that exits is God and nothing else can exist.

God's very nature is one of wholeness, oneness. He cannot be divided. He cannot be separated. He is unlimited and is all that is, so all that is, is unlimited. As God's creation, we are also unlimited.

Where one speck of God exists, all of God is.

When He created us, He shared His very being with us and His ultimate gift to us is that He shared Himself fully. God extended the fullness of Himself into us and even though we may think we are this perishable form of a body, at our essence we are the creative spirit of God.

God's greatest gift to us was not just life,
But life as God knew it.

Everything God is, we are. There is nothing God is that we are not.

As humans, we tend to think that God is bigger, better and more powerful than we are. One reason we think this is because of the connotation of the word "creation." We think of the one who creates as being greater than his/her creation.

From God's perspective, He sees Himself as our creator and he knows us as Himself. There is no difference in the mind of God. And since our mind is the extension of God's mind as us, in our mind is all of the creative power of God. We are the fullness, the wholeness, the oneness of God. God knows us as Himself because that's the way He created us.

Why do we have trouble believing this?

The human race thinks that when someone gives you something, then they no longer have it. Our five senses tell us this is true. If one person gives a dollar to another then the receiver has the dollar but the giver doesn't. We believe that once something is given it is gone. It cannot be in both places. So then, that belief makes it difficult for us to believe that God could give us the fullness of Himself. If He did that then we would be powerful, loving, abundant and omnipresent, but God would not. So then, how could He still be God?

There is, however, one thing that circumvents that belief. There is one thing that one man can give to another man and still not lose it. That one thing is a thought or an idea. Ideas have been shared for millenniums from one person to another. One person has an idea then shares it with someone else. Now they both have the same idea.

It does not diminish the thought or the thinker for an idea to be shared. In fact, when an idea is shared, it only increases the energy of the thought and the thinker. It's the same with God. God created man in his mind. We are an idea, a thought, of God. It did not diminish God or us when God created us.

We humans also have trouble with the belief that we are made of God because we think we are a body and our bodies seem so frail. Oh, sure, we have all been taught that we are really a soul but this whole business of being a soul yet having a body is quite confusing to us.

We see ourselves as a body every day when we look in the mirror; we refer to each other as bodies as we interact with other people in a myriad of ways, all involving the body in one way or the other. We get sick, we experience discomfort, we hurt ourselves physically, and we watch other people die. Basically, as we go about our lives we consciously or unconsciously see ourselves as a body.

Once the idea that we are a body has lodged in our minds over years of experiencing life this way, it is no wonder that we don't naturally think of, or see ourselves, as an expression of God's energy.

Everything about how we see ourselves screams out limitation to us in one way or the other. We have all done an exquisite job of weaving our belief system into a bedrock of beliefs that we are a body and therefore limited.

The truth is that we are not our bodies. We are powerful energy that has no limits just like God. The body is not eternal but we are because we are as infinite as God is. The body will only be here with us while we are on the Earth. The body dies but we never will.

We are energy, God's energy. Our energy has no limits and it is certainly not limited to being in our bodies. The God energy that we are, the beingness that God created, is as eternal and as powerful as He is. As long as we insist on identifying with our bodies, we will circumvent our true identity and limit ourselves in a myriad of ways.

The more we identify with our bodies, the more confused we seem to get about our identities. We're not sure who we are or who God is. As we start to identify with our bodies, the more we become curious about our bodies and become less curious about the God energy that we really are. More and more we start to learn about our bodies and less and less we start to know about God. As we start to know less and less about God we get totally confused about our true identity. We don't know the reality of ourselves because we don't know God but we know in infinite detail all about our bodies.

The more we identify with our bodies, the more certain we become that we are separate from God since it doesn't seem like He is part of our frail bodies that get sick and die. We start to think of God as being "out there" and ourselves as being "in here", contained inside our bodies.

Our reality is that we are not contained anywhere. We are God's energy that is not separate from Him and therefore we are everywhere as He is. We are everything that He is. We go on into infinity as He does.

The more we identify with our bodies, the greater our terror becomes. The human body appears to us as limited and frail. After all, doesn't the body get hurt and die and aren't we limited by not being able to walk through walls or on water? If we see ourselves as a body, we must also see ourselves as separate from God. Therefore, in our frailty and limitedness, we must be at the mercy of God for survival.

To make matters worse, the more we identify with our bodies and our terror increases, we build countless defense systems within the framework of our thoughts. We substitute the truth about ourselves with monuments of defense. We terrorize and exhaust ourselves in trying to protect something that needs absolutely no defense or protection.

The more we identify with our bodies, the more certain we become that our fellow man is separate from us. We can see our own bodies and we can see other people's bodies and therefore we draw the conclusion that we are separate. We see the boundaries of our skin and we think that what is within our skin is "us" and what is within the skin of other bodies is "them." But if we look beyond bodies to our true identities, we see everyone as powerful energy, all created by

God from His own energy. God's energy can't be divided, separated or limited in any way. The truth is we are all one energy, God's energy.

So why did God create us?

Creativity always wants to be expressed. So God created us as a creative expression of Himself.

He created us from the fullness of Himself so that He could experience Himself as us.

He cannot see us as different from Himself because God created us literally from Himself, out of His own energy. In His eyes there is only oneness. Everything is the same to Him because it is all Him. He does not see Himself as separate from us. He is experiencing everything we experience.

We are God's energy experiencing life as a human being.

In giving man the fullness of Himself, including His full creative power, God intended that we then go out and use that power to also create. What God intended for us to create was what He willed for us: abundance, peace, love, fulfillment, beauty, success, health and freedom. God intended that we create as He had created. He intended that we express Him and His nature through our creations.

*God created us so that He would be
able to experience Himself as us
and He gave us the fullness of Himself
so that we would be able to experience
ourselves as Him.*

It sounds very arrogant and sacrilegious to think that I am the fullness of God in human form. How does God see it?

God does not see it as arrogant for us to see ourselves as the fullness of Him. Quite the contrary, it is much more arrogant to see ourselves not as He created us.

*Neither God, nor His creation, can ever be
changed in any way. When His creation creates,
it is always of and as God.*

Humans have forgotten who and what they are and have made up an imaginary self, encased in an imaginary body, living in what seems to be a physical world and universe. The ancient traditions called this "illusion." Contemporary culture calls it "God's creation." Nothing can be created outside of God.

Then how can we have bodies and live on Earth in a physical universe?

God's mind is unlimited and so is yours. At the beginning of what humans call "time", there was a moment when His creation, the original you, or "You", wondered what it would be like to create something that it was not.

In that moment, the illusion of being separated from your Source was made up in your mind. That was an imaginary idea that was not of God. It was not real, it just seemed so. What you make up in your mind, you believe is so. That was true then and is true now.

In that moment of believing you had separated from God, you now believed there were two things: God and you. From that moment forward, in what you call time, everything you have made up is a reflection of your original belief that you have separated from God. From that belief, everything you have ever made up about yourself and the physical universe has opposite qualities: life and death, good and bad, right and wrong, health and sickness, happy and sad, beginning and end.

God has no beginning and no end.

Since God's creation is His extension of Himself into and as you, which is really You, you cannot end, you cannot die, you cannot have pain. You are as God created you and will always be.

Then what about us having bodies and living in a physical universe?

The terror of you believing you separated from God caused you to make up the physical universe in your mind, as a way of hiding from God. There began your opposites: the spirit of God, which is also your spirit, and the physical universe.

Also in that same instant, you, the one creation, split your mind into countless pieces and each hid in bodies so as to never be found by God. There again came your opposites: the oneness of God and all the separate parts of God that you know as human bodies.

That same one instant also produced in your mind the belief in the "original sin" that you had actually left God and were now a separate being split into countless other separate beings. God is incapable of sin. As God's creation, so are you. If you had truly sinned, you would have truly separated from God, but you did not. You are, and will always be, as God created you. You are living in and as an illusion.

The collective you put all of this into motion and as you split into your countless aspects you repressed it all, hid it all away in the deepest recesses of your mind, never to be remembered, because the terror of it was impossible to bear.

Born now was perception, belief, judgment, all based on sin, guilt and fear, with all of their opposites, instead of the true knowing of the oneness of love or, more correctly, Love.

This is the world you now see and experience. The inner you, your Godness, has been pulling you back home since the beginning of time. However, you can only receive the gift of truth with an open mind and yours, the collective made-up separate mind, split off into the countless aspects of the one original illusion, has been closed through the medium of thought, perception, belief and judgment as you have used your separated mind to try to make a heaven on earth.

It is much more arrogant to see ourselves small when God created us large. It is much more arrogant to see ourselves poor when He created us to live in abundance. It is much more arrogant to see ourselves weak when He created us with unlimited power. It is much more arrogant to see ourselves as unloved when we are not and never have been separated from unconditional love. It is much more arrogant to see ourselves separate from the way He created us.

Arrogance is substituting our belief of who we are for the way God really created us.

If God is not within us, then God never existed.
—Voltaire

Know ye not…that the spirit of God dwelleth within you?
—I Corinthians 3:16

You have everything in you that Buddha has, that Christ has. You've got it all. But only when you start to acknowledge it is it going to get interesting. Your problem is you're afraid to acknowledge your own beauty. You're too busy holding on to your own unworthiness. You'd rather be a schnook sitting before some great man. That fits in more with who you think you are. Well, enough already. I sit before you and I look and I see your beauty, even if you don't.
—Ram Dass

The purpose is to identify not with the body which is falling away, but with the consciousness of which it is a vehicle. This is something I learned from my myths. Am I the bulb that carries the light, or am I the light of which the bulb is the vehicle? If you can identify with the consciousness, you can watch this thing go like an old car. There goes the fender, etc. But it's expected; and then gradually the whole thing drops off and consciousness rejoins consciousness. I live with these myths—and they tell me to do this, to identify with the Christ or the Shiva in me. And that doesn't die, it resurrects. It is an essential experience of any mystical realization that you die to your flesh and are born to your spirit. You identify with the consciousness in life—and that is the god.

—Joseph Campbell

Chapter 2

Heaven on Earth

*Your pain is in the breaking of the shell
that encloses your understanding.*
—Kahlil Gibran

By meditating for days on end we were able to keep ourselves from getting depressed about our situation. But it was hard. It had been two months and our stocks kept falling and we were dangerously close to getting a margin call from our broker. For those of you who don't speak "stock market" that means we would've had a choice of coming up with more money (which we didn't have) or selling the stock at a very low price.

With the stock market, nothing is ever gained or lost until the buy/sell transaction is complete. It is only a gain or loss "on paper."

We knew that if we sold our stocks at the bottom that the loss would be realized and we would be worse off financially. Or at least that is what we thought.

The hardest part for us was believing what we were being told in our meditations. It's hard to believe that you are the fullness of God when you are worried about getting a margin call. It's hard to think that you are full of God energy when you feel so helpless, afraid and frustrated. So we began to question the dichotomy between being God and the way we were feeling, thinking and living.

If we are God, then why do our lives seem so imperfect and painful sometimes?

When God created us, He gave us the fullness of Himself. That meant that He also gave us free will and the ability to create whatever we desired. We created alongside God and experienced what it was like to be all powerful, omnipotent, omnipresent, infinitely peaceful, lavishly abundant and totally free.

One moment, using our infinite creativity, we curiously decided to experience what it was like to not be and have all of those things. Using our creativity, we created the experience of being separate from God. We weren't separate; we just created the experience of separateness in our minds.

The experience of separation brought up a new emotion for us. It was our first moment of feeling fear. Before that, we had only experienced joy and laughter. But in that moment of fear and seriousness, we forgot that the separation was only in our minds. We thought it was real.

The fear and separation that we felt in that moment was like a pin prick in a fabric. The more we paid attention to the fear and feeling of separation, the bigger it became until we created a huge hole in the fabric of our lives called fear. This separateness that we felt then and still feel today is the source of all fear in our lives. If we realized our oneness with God, there would be no fear. It is only in separation that fear exists.

We are afraid because we believe we are separate from God.

Fear, then, becomes the texture or the fabric from which we make up our lives. Being afraid, we then want protection so we create a whole set of beliefs that we think will protect us. This set of beliefs is commonly called the ego or some people call them false beliefs.

This set of beliefs relates to what we eat, where we go, how we behave, our vocation, who we marry, how we raise our children, and literally everything else in our lives.

We have created our own beliefs, or accepted our parent's version of beliefs, concerning everything in our lives based on the lie that we are separate from God. If we believed we were one with God, it wouldn't matter what we ate, or where we went or how we behaved or who we married or anything else.

In the reality of our oneness with God,
nothing and no one can hurt us,
limit us, or keep us from expressing
our God energy.

These false beliefs soon take on a life of their own because we take our natural God power and give it to these beliefs. The only power these beliefs really have is the power we give to them by believing in them. We actually give life to our false beliefs by placing the power of our minds and emotions solidly behind them. Having placed all of our power behind these beliefs, we become convinced that they are more powerful than we are and that we need to obey these beliefs in order to protect ourselves.

Having created a set of beliefs that we have endowed with the false ability to take care of us, we do everything we can to ensure that those beliefs endure. Those beliefs, in turn, continually reinforce themselves by attracting circumstances that will keep us in fear. Without fear, after all, we wouldn't need these beliefs (our ego) to take care of us.

We have a constant, unspoken sense of nakedness and vulnerability within us because underneath it all, we believe we are separate from God. So when any of the constructs of our ego are challenged, we respond voraciously with every ounce of our energy to protect our egos.

We all have our conscious and unconscious minds wired with

these ego beliefs that we think keep us safe and we don't want these beliefs to go away because then we might feel unsafe and maybe even terrified. So we constantly reinforce old beliefs and constantly create new beliefs that we think will protect us. But instead of protecting us, these beliefs create more fear and limitation in our lives.

The only way out of this madness is to realize that the separation from God that we think is there is not really there. If we are one with God, there is no need to defend or protect because God cannot be hurt or diminished in any way.

Our realization of our oneness with God is our heaven on earth. Our defense of our perceived separation from God is our hell on earth.

Why do our fears seem to be justified?

Fear is not real because separation from God is not real. We just think it is.

Although love, the one Love of God that we all are, has no real opposite, we are always either in love or in fear, which means in truth or in illusion.

There is a way to see every situation from the vantage point of love.

Love has no fear because love sees only love. God is love. We are love. God sees only what is real and only what God created is real. God did not create poverty or lack or weakness or hate. Since we are as God created us, we can see as God does.

When we were created we were given the full creative power of God. And we create every moment just like God, with our thoughts, feelings and beliefs which is how we perceive the world and make judgments about ourself, other people and how the world works.

When we entertained the thought of separateness, we created thoughts of fear. These thoughts of fear created a world for us filled with hunger, animosity, lack, deprivation, anger, jealousy, and blame.

This world that we created is not real because we created it from fear instead of love. When we create from fear we use our creative energy to create an illusion that looks real but is not.

We created this world from our false beliefs and not from the truth of our Godness.

We created this world from the false belief that we are separate from God, which is not true.

Only what is created from love and truth is real and the world we see before us with our five senses is not reality. Our reality is our Godness. Our reality is love not fear.

When we ask to be delivered from poverty, God sees only abundance so it is as if He doesn't know what we are talking about. He sees us only in the unlimited abundance with which He created us.

When we see poverty in our lives, we need to understand that its manifestation into our physical world is a result of a false belief in financial lack and underneath that, a belief in separation from God.

When we feel afraid the best thing we can do is to try to look at the situation with God's eyes. We can ask ourselves what thoughts we are having that God would never have. Those are the thoughts that make fear seem to be justified. We can also ask what thoughts God would have in the same situation that we are not thinking. Those are the thoughts of love.

Our fears seem to be justified because what we have created with our sense of separateness from God is a view of ourselves as something we are not. We basically believe we are the exact opposite of God. Instead of believing in truth, we believe in the illusion that we are something that we are not. There is no comfort in this, only hidden terror.

Our defense systems of false beliefs that have been created over the ages have created a sense of self that is not real. Everything in the world is a threat to this false sense of self unless everything in each person's world is absolutely perfect all of the time. Since our world is based on illusion, the only perfection is the underlying truth that we are all avoiding.

By believing in a self that is based on illusion, the very definition of ego, all thoughts of truth are a direct affront to who we believe we are. In our minds, truth is a threat to our very existence. The feeling of leaving fear for truth is a feeling of fear bordering on terror.

We defend our false selves with an elaborate system of defense based on false beliefs. At our deepest levels of consciousness, we believe we are fighting for our very lives. In reality, by holding onto our false beliefs, we are continuing to create the exact opposite of who we really are. This is why our fears seem to be justified.

We are not who we think we are.
We are far greater than that.
We are the unlimited essence of
God who created us. We share
that essence with all of creation.

How can I recognize thoughts as false beliefs?

Anything having to do with fear is a false belief. That is, it doesn't come from the truth of God's creation. Thoughts attacking our worth are from false beliefs. Our worth was established by God when we were created and nothing and no one can change that.

Do you see here what a relief that is? We don't have to try anymore to bolster our egos with more false beliefs about how good or right we are. We can simply let go of fear and what will come to the surface of our consciousness is love.

However, unless your mind is in 100% certainty about this, which it will eventually be, you may feel an aversion to letting go of fear because it seems like you're letting go of your very self. But that self is a false self and, with enough practice, you will begin to feel and know the certainty of who and what you are as you let go of fear and allow love to bubble up from within the depths of your being to the awareness of your consciousness.

Now back to recognizing thoughts as false beliefs. Thoughts having to do with self-praise or specialness are generally from false beliefs. Since we think we are separated from God we like to compare ourselves with each other to set ourselves apart and be seen somehow as better than someone else. We tend to only want to be around other people that we think are "like us" and avoid other people who are not "like us."

God created all of us from Himself and He sees only equality and sameness. Thoughts having to do with any kind of comparison between ourselves and others stems from false beliefs. How could God entertain thoughts of comparison when He sees only Himself everywhere He looks?

Thoughts having to do with anything that is opposite of the nature of God, like lack or deprivation, are from false beliefs. Neither God, nor His creations, lack anything.

Thoughts glorifying the body are from false beliefs. The body is not who we are. How could we compare the grandeur of God, our

Godness or God energy, to our bodies? Even if it is what society calls "a good body" it is still nothing compared to our Godness.

Our ego thoughts center on the belief that our bodies are frail and vulnerable. If our ego can keep us believing that we are a body, not God's energy, then because our body is frail and vulnerable, we will need the ego for protection. If our false beliefs can convince us that we are just a body we will forever be married to their well-thought-out plan for protection.

Thoughts of judgment are from ego. God cannot and does not judge. He created everything from Himself and to judge anything would be to judge Himself.

Only the ego judges.

Thoughts of guilt are just another form of judgment. And, even worse, they emanate from our original guilt that we separated from God that we keep deeply hidden from ourselves.

Guilt is a special type of judgment that we level at ourselves designed to tear us down and make us feel badly about ourselves. Then, because we feel weak, the ego once again can show us that we need it.

In God's eyes, we are seen only as blameless and innocent, period.

Thoughts of negativity and failure are from false beliefs. God is only about fulfillment and success. There is nothing that cannot be accomplished by the Godness within us.

Thoughts that relive the past are from false beliefs. Our belief that we are a separate self, separate from God and separate from everyone and everything else began with the false belief that we left God in the past and have to face the future alone. Eternity has no opposite. But our belief in the past and future is what made up time.

So we become convinced by looking at the past that the past determines the future. Thus the ego ensures that we will need it in the future and therefore it endures.

Any thoughts of limitation are false beliefs. We are a thought of God and as long as His thought didn't limit us, then we are not limited. It is only our own limiting thoughts that limit us.

Our false beliefs (our ego) are diametrically opposed to our true energy, which is God. For most of us, this makes it seem like we have two opposing voices in our head, one from our Godness and one from our false beliefs.

One voice is love and the other is fear. If you recognize fear, choose love. If you recognize love, keep choosing it. Love never disguises itself. It is like truth, simple and pure.

Fear is most often disguised and its disguises can be quite intricate and extremely subtle. That is why false beliefs are sometimes very confusing because confusion is one of fear's disguises.

If we can't recognize which voice we are hearing, God or ego, then we can at least reject whatever we are thinking and invite God's thoughts to enter. God's thoughts are truth and truth will not come uninvited.

Fear is a choice we make and, by inference, it is a declaration for truth and love not to enter. But if you are determined to see and hear truth it cannot help but bring itself to your awareness. Do you feel the comfort of what this is saying? When you decide for truth, you are no longer blocking it and it will come to you in just the very way that you can best receive it.

Where did these false beliefs (my ego) come from?

Most of our false beliefs were passed down from generation to generation. But as adults, we have generated, reinforced or at least passively accepted our conscious and unconscious beliefs. The good news is that we also have the power to change anything within our belief system that we don't like. So if we want to heal our perceived separation from God we just need to be on guard against beliefs that stem from fear and separation.

Why do my false beliefs feel so powerful?

Our false beliefs feel so powerful because the roots of them have been embedded in human consciousness since the beginning of time. The human race has developed an entire structure of thinking that can be referred to as human or race consciousness. It is all based on the false belief that we are separate from God.

From this original false belief, mankind has produced countless other false beliefs, all designed to protect us from the fear of the original false belief. This is the basis of our human race consciousness. It has the power of millenniums of thinking behind it. It has the power of generation after generation teaching and handing down belief after belief, all designed to protect family and children from our perceived frailties of being human and from the limitations we perceive about the world.

All of these beliefs are false but they are very strong. Our very identities are based on them. They are built into the thinking of the human race and they are powerful.

What are the consequences of maintaining my false beliefs?

Every false belief that we keep hidden is a direct assault on the truth of what God created. The two are diametrically opposed. Our false beliefs can not hurt or change the truth of our Godness but they can limit our ability to tap into our Godness and therefore limit the amount of healing that we have the power to extend to ourselves and others.

Truth is where joy and happiness reside because truth and love are inseparable. When we choose to live in the truth of how God created us, we live in love, joy and happiness. The appearances in our lives that seem to contradict this joy and happiness are not real because they were created from fear and not love. They were created from our past beliefs in fear.

We can create from love this moment and therefore change the appearances in our lives to reflect love instead of fear. We can create from love this moment and watch the appearances in our lives start to reflect the attributes of God.

The things we create from fear may seem pleasant and pleasurable in the moment, but all things created from fear eventually end in pain and suffering. Whatever aspect of our lives that relates to our false beliefs will, at a minimum, produce some sort of discomfort for us. It will be manifest in our bodies, emotions, relationships, livelihood and other areas of our lives that relate to that belief. Creating from fear can only produce pain and creating from love is the only way out.

Doesn't it seem rather insane to deny what I am sensing with my five senses is real?

It only seems that way to us.

***To God, it is insane to believe more
in our five senses than to believe
in the reality of what He created.***

Our dream world that we visit every night is a parallel to truth and reality. When we wake up every morning, we are not still frightened of the characters and situations that we experienced in our dream during the night. That is because when we wake up, we realize it was just a dream. Sometimes we are so enmeshed in the dream that it seems real and in that state we can't change the dream, or awaken from it. But if we awaken even a little bit out of the dream, we can re-dream it and change the characters and situations that we don't like.

Life on earth is much the same. What we create from love and truth is real. Everything else we create is like a dream. It is really just an illusion. There's nothing to be afraid of because, like a dream, the situations and characters are not real. If we don't become too mired in the dream world believing it is real, we can change anything not to our liking. We can simply re-dream it.

We can tell if we are enmeshed in the dream or not. When we find ourselves in circumstances that we don't like and we start changing our thoughts and emotions and we realize that by doing so we are, in fact, changing the circumstances of the dream, then we are not enmeshed. The fact that circumstances can be changed at all tells us it is a dream.

But when our thoughts and emotions start to be influenced by the dream, instead of the other way around, we've become mired in the dream. The way to tell if we are mired in the dream or not is to ask ourselves, "Who has the power, me or the dream?" If the dream has the power, then we need to reacquaint ourselves with the truth of who we are.

When we create from fear, we create an illusion that matches it. Just like a dream, our illusions fall away when the light of truth shines on them. When we harbor thoughts and beliefs about lack, we create a physical form that looks real to our five senses but is really more like a dream or an illusion.

When we discover the truth about our abundance and we replace our belief in lack with a belief in abundance, we start to create something real. Even though we might be creating an illusory form, like a new car or new house or more money or a healthy body, our underlying energy is in truth.

One way to tell the difference between illusion and reality is that illusions are changeable and truth is not. Our illusions that we create are just like dreams. The fact that we can change our physical circumstances shows us that they are illusions.

***What is real is what God created
and only what God created is real.***

It doesn't feel like we're creating anything so how is it that we create?

When God created us, He gave us His full creative power. And that creative power is always at work every moment in everyone. It is truly a gift because that power is constantly at work attracting into physical form all the things that our emotions, thoughts, words, beliefs, decisions and desires direct it to create.

It has to create because that is the nature of the Godness within each of us. It can be no other way. It's a gift that most of us have yet to discover. We forgot we had it. At some point since we were created, we stopped consciously using our creative powers and just like everything else in our lives, when we stopped using it, we forgot that we had it.

It feels to us like we are not creating because we have been doing it unconsciously. It is natural to us like breathing. We don't even realize that we are doing it. We seem so puzzled by what we have created in our lives so far because so much of our emotional and mental framework is hidden even to ourselves.

Our emotional and mental framework comes from contact with other emotional and mental frameworks. The TV shows we watch, ads in magazines, strangers we watch, conversations with loved ones and meetings at work are all examples of contacts we make with other belief systems.

Those beliefs that stay with us are those beliefs and impressions we internalize into our own belief system. Thus, a passing comment by a stranger will most likely be experienced in the moment and then released, but a harsh criticism by a boss will most likely be taken in and internalized.

How it is internalized is up to us. We can internalize it as "I'm no good" or we can internalize it as "My boss was having a bad day." Most of us feel safest by internalizing beliefs that our families and society embrace as well (there's safety in numbers). Unfortunately, our society's belief system is based on separation from God and therefore a system of false beliefs.

We must learn to think positively when all around us is negativity, think abundance when all we see is lack, think peace when we are taught to think of war and attack and think health when the threat of sickness is all around us. We must get used to our creative powers and realize that there is a direct correlation between what we think and believe and what appears in our physical world.

God's power within us doesn't judge our thoughts or what it is we want it to create. It's our life. That is what we call free will. If we choose to hold on to a belief about lack or suffering, that is what our Divine creative power will create for us in our life.

All of the universe works using the laws of cause and effect. What we think about, feel about, and/or make decisions about is the cause. And the effects are what we see with our five senses out in the world. The absolute best thing we can do for ourselves is first to know ourselves and be aware of the thoughts, emotions and desires within us.

The second best thing we can do is to then take responsibility for what we have already created in our life. The more we try to blame another person or situation for our circumstances, the more we are cutting ourselves off from using the most powerful force in the universe to better our lives. Blaming another person or situation affirms our helplessness and therefore short-circuits our power.

If we can take a look at what kinds of beliefs, emotions, words, thoughts, decisions and desires we are putting out, we will see the connection to what we have created. Once we have discovered that connection, if we don't like what we've created, we can change it by changing our emotions, thoughts, beliefs and desires. We're the boss here. No one else can tell us what to create in our lives. It is a wondrous gift and it is the source of all our safety, abundance, health, and power.

God is love. His plan for creation can only be rooted in love. Does not that simple thought, rather than erudite reasonings, offer solace to the human heart?
—Paramahansa Yogananda

The function of dreams is to teach the waking mind how to forget what it thinks it knows but doesn't.
—William R. Stinson

Man is made by his belief. As he believes, so he is.
—Bhagavad Gita

You are in physical existence to learn and understand that your energy, translated into feelings, thoughts and emotions causes all your experiences. There are no exceptions.
—Seth

There are no accidents whatsoever in the universe.
—Ram Dass

Chapter 3

Spiritual Eyes

*One has not only an ability to perceive the world
but an ability to alter one's perception of it; more simply, one can
change things by the manner in which one looks at them.*
—Tom Robbins

We ended up closely missing a margin call (by 1%) and some of our stocks started slowly going up in price again. We were even able to get unstuck out of one of them which helped us to pay back some of the money we owed to our broker.

Even with these minor financial miracles, we still knew we weren't living life in the abundant manner that God intended. We also knew that our underlying beliefs were responsible for those financial limitations. We understood that as those beliefs began to change, so would our financial situation.

We became diligent in releasing our false beliefs that were blocking the manifestation of what we wanted. We became determined to allow God to substitute His beliefs in their place. The area we knew needed the most work was our financial situation. We obviously had some limiting false beliefs about money.

We realized that focusing on our false beliefs would only emphasize them more. It became clear to us that we needed clarity about what it was we really wanted to see happen in our lives. That would give us a shift in focus and we believed that by focusing on what we wanted, all the while releasing false beliefs and the thoughts and emotions relating to them, we would attract exactly what it was that we wanted.

What we found when we searched our hearts for our true desires (as opposed to whims), was that everything we wanted essentially related to an attribute of God. We knew we weren't living abundantly and we wanted to. Abundance is an attribute of God. We also knew that we weren't living with any financial consistency and we wanted to. Consistency and certainty are attributes of God. So, the essence of what we wanted was to live with consistent abundance.

There were three forms of this consistent abundance that we wanted to see manifested in our physical world.

First, we wanted to be out of debt. To us, that meant paying back all margin debt to our broker and paying off our mortgage.

Secondly, we wanted our stocks to get back to a profitable situation.

Thirdly, we wanted a consistent income in our lives and we knew therefore that this probably couldn't come from the stock market because there is too much volatility in the market for there to be consistency.

We decided to look at these forms as goals but everything we wanted boiled down to wanting to live with consistent abundance.

We meditated, visualized, prayed and used affirmations every day on all the things we wanted to see manifested in our lives and on the essence of living with consistent abundance. We also consciously watched our thoughts to discover the false beliefs that were holding us back.

One of the most significant false beliefs we discovered related to who or what was our source for prosperity. Without really consciously thinking about it, we realized that we had adopted a false belief that our paychecks were the source of our abundance. In other words, we saw our employers as the source of our wealth and therefore our employers were our security.

After we quit working in corporate America, we believed that the stock market was the source of our wealth. We realized that we had placed all of our security in this world on our employer or the vehicle through which most of our money was supplied. We also discovered that we saw money itself as our source of wealth and security.

It was very scary to let go of this false belief because it meant that we had to quit rationally trying to figure out how to acquire money to live on and we just had to trust the Godness within us to manifest our natural abundance.

We had set some lofty financial goals for ourselves and we had no idea how they would be accomplished, yet we knew we needed to trust that they would be.

What is the source of all good things coming in to my life?

When we were created, God gave us the fullness of Himself. He has nothing left to give to us. We already have it all. He gave us all of Himself and He is everything and there is nothing He is not.

In His thought of us, there is no separation between Him and us. In His eyes, we are one with Him. Therefore, He sees us as already being and having everything. When we ask to be healed from poverty or sickness or deprivation of any kind, God simply doesn't see it. He sees us the way He created us, with the fullness of Himself within us.

God has essentially passed on the baton of creation. It's now up to us. The gift of His full creative power allows us to create whatever we want on this earth. This divinity within us is truly the source of anything and everything we want.

When we see a job, or the stock market, or a spouse, or a bank account as our source of abundance and therefore our security in this world, we short circuit our divine power. We take our God-given divine creative power and hand it over to something or someone else. Several things happen when we do this.

First, we create for ourselves another god. We assign power to something other than the Godness within us so that now we think there is something outside of us that has power over us. It doesn't really have power over us but we give it our power by believing it has power.

So to us, it now seems like we are powerless and a false belief of powerlessness forms. This false belief then creates powerlessness in our lives and it becomes a vicious cycle. The more powerless we feel, the more we think we need to depend on this outside source to provide abundance for us.

Secondly, when we view something outside of ourselves as our source, we immediately create fear in our lives because outside sources can be taken away. We all run around being scared of losing our jobs, our mates, or our money because we see those things as our source of security. We feel afraid because we can get fired from jobs, the stock market can fall, spouses can die and unexpected expenses can wipe out bank accounts. So we end up living our lives in powerlessness and fear.

Lastly, by seeing something outside of us as our source, we limit our abundance because no matter how great a job is or how large a bank account is, nothing can compare to the unlimited abundance and prosperity the Godness within us wants to express through us. This is true not only about abundance but also about love, safety, or anything else we might want. The Godness within us is our only real source for everything.

Why does it seem easier to see our jobs and bank accounts as our source rather than God?

One reason stems from the way the human race is socialized. We are taught that only what we see, hear, touch, taste, and smell is real. Nothing else is real. Jobs are visible to the human eye. Money and spouses are also visible. The source within us is invisible to the human eye. We can only see it with our spiritual eyes.

Our spiritual eyes are developed by
exchanging our false beliefs for truth and
then by living our life having faith in that truth.

We think it doesn't make sense to deny our five senses but God thinks it doesn't make sense to deny what He created. To God, it makes perfect sense to deny the ugliness we have created in this physical world and believe in what He created for us.

Another reason it seems easier to see something outside of ourselves as our source is that our power is so great that it literally scares us to think about using it. Think about something very powerful, a tornado, a hurricane, an earthquake or maybe a volcano. However powerful those things seem, our power is greater.

We literally have the same power as God because we are His energy. For most of us that is a scary thought. To believe that we have so much power scares us because we are afraid we don't know how to handle it. And if we accept that we have that kind of power then we also have to accept responsibility for everything we have already created in our lives. We have all misused the power we have been given and created poverty, disharmony, loneliness, and unhappiness in our lives. So, we would much rather think of someone or something else outside of us as having that power so that we don't have to face the responsibility that goes along with having that power.

This belief seems so ingrained in me. How can I change it?

Money is not our source of abundance. Neither are jobs. It seems like our belief in them as our source is ingrained in us because it is. Very few human beings are raised without being programmed to think that the more money we have, the more powerful we are and, therefore, the more secure we are in this world. Then as we grow up, we transfer that thought to jobs, spouses and other vehicles that flow money to us. We start to see our job or our spouse or maybe the stock market as our source of abundance.

Unfortunately, the lies that money equates with power and power gives us security have been told so much that the entire human race believes them. When beliefs are deeply ingrained, the best way to change them is just to be willing to change them.

If we fight against a belief, we only make it stronger because we see it as powerful and something to be struggled with.

Anything we see as something to be struggled with becomes powerful in our eyes and we short-circuit our own God-given power. The best space to start with is just to be willing to see things differently. As we are willing to let go of the false belief, the Godness within us will be glad to have its voice of truth heard.

Many people think it is hard to release a certain false belief because they identify with it so strongly. Even our words show this. We say, "I am angry" not "I am feeling anger." But emotions, thoughts and beliefs are not us. Many people think they are their emotions and thoughts because they think they need them to define themselves.

The real definition of each of us is so far superior than any emotion or thought we could ever have or think. God gave us that definition when He created us and it has never changed. Try seeing all emotions, thoughts and beliefs as helium balloons that we carry around with us. As we see one that we would like to change, we simply let go of the cord and watch it float away. Then we turn our attention to our Godness within and ask that God's belief replace the one we let go of. If the old belief tries to float back into our awareness, we simply give it no attention.

If God is my source, how do I know I'm creating what He wants me to create? How do I know I'm not misusing the source?

As humans, we are so afraid of God's will. We think that His will gives us the opposite of what we want. We think submitting to God's will automatically infers pain, suffering and sacrifice. What we don't realize is that God's will cannot go against His nature. God could never use His will to contradict His nature. His nature is one of love, overflowing abundance, creativity, fulfillment, beauty, limitlessness, joy, harmony, peace and power.

His will for us is that we experience these same things. God wills love for us. God wills that we live in overflowing abundance. God wills for us everything He is and has. That is why He gave us the fullness of Himself. Having given us the fullness of Himself, that also included His will. Since His will for us is abundance, creativity, fulfillment, beauty, limitlessness, joy, harmony, peace and power, what else is there that we could want? When we trace our desires down to their core, their very essence, our desires relate to the nature of God.

We want for our lives what God has already willed for us.

In other words, whatever we want is God's will. He sees no difference. He sees our will and His as one. So God wants for us everything we want for ourselves. What's more, He has already given us everything that we want. We just have to align our will with what He has already willed for us. We can be assured that when we align our desires with the attributes of God then we are creating for ourselves what He intended us to create and we are not misusing the source.

How do I learn to trust the invisible source inside me as my supply of everything I want and need?

The first step is being willing to let go of seeing anything else as our source. If we can do that, our Godness will take over and demonstrate to us how well it can provide for anything we want and need.

The Godness within each of us listens to all of our thoughts, emotions, beliefs, desires and needs. Its job is then to create for us in physical form what we have established that we want.

We don't have to worry about how to accomplish what we want. Our job is to keep our thoughts and emotions focused on the attribute of God that we desire to see in physical form and give no attention to any fearful thoughts, beliefs or emotions.

The kingdom of God is within you…Seek ye first the kingdom of God and all things will be added unto you.
—Jesus

Man was born to be rich, or grow rich by the use of his faculties, by the union of thought with nature.
—Emerson

What lies before us, and what lies behind us, are tiny matters compared to what is within us.
—Emerson

Chapter 4

Innocent and Blameless

You can't solve a problem on the same level it was created. You have to rise above it to the next level.
—Albert Einstein

We were able to sell several of our stocks with either a profit or a small loss. That gave us enough money to pay off our margin debt completely (one of our financial goals) and we even ended up with a small amount of money to begin trading stocks again.

Unfortunately, it seemed like everything we touched went sour. We kept trying to figure out new ways of trading that would solve the problem. We tried day trading (a system of trading where you hold stocks for very short periods of time) and that didn't work for us. We tried just about any new system that we could think of since we still weren't making any money. Nothing seemed to work for us. We kept trying to fix the problem by changing what we were doing and taking a different course of action.

We realized that changing our actions wasn't working and somewhere along the way we also noticed that we were still seeing ourselves as victims of the stock market and we were seeing the powerful people on Wall Street as our enemies. We bashed everyone and everything associated with the stock market. We cursed Alan Greenspan (the head of the Federal Reserve at the time) because he kept raising interest rates. We hurled animosity against the analysts who downgraded our stocks. In short, we still weren't taking responsibility for creating our own financial mess.

We also noticed that everyone we knew that was a trader stayed in a very negative and fearful energy. All the market news was "what we should be worried about" or "what the next crisis would be." We began to question whether this was really the right livelihood for us.

Barbara, who is not very comfortable with being bombarded by other people's fear, stopped trading altogether and decided just to meditate, pray, write on this book and journal. Jimmie just kept trying to fix the problem with a new course of action. Both of us had developed a lot of judgment towards the market and the people that make up the market.

We finally realized that if we saw the stock market as a terrible ruse for rich people to steal money from people like us then that is exactly what we would create for ourselves. We discovered that whatever we believed about any situation, institution or person would be projected out into the universe and it would be reflected back to us with a physical form that exactly matched the vibration of the belief.

In other words, if we saw the market as a cheating, manipulating system that sucked people's money from them, then that is exactly what we would get—all of our money sucked from us. We also realized that our five senses had been trained to only see, hear, feel, taste and touch in accordance with our beliefs. Essentially, we saw what we believed we would see. We heard what we believed we would hear and so on. So if we believed in a manipulating, unfair stock market, which is all we would see with our physical eyes and hear with our physical ears.

We had known for awhile that the way we saw ourselves and God was important to our lives but we finally realized that the way we see the world and everyone in it is equally important. Once again the solution to our financial problems came down to changing false beliefs. This time these beliefs revolved around how we saw our fellow man and our physical world.

What is God's view of our physical world?

God sees only harmony, cooperation, innocence, abundance and love. That is because that is how He created us. We are the ones who, in feeling separate from Him, created fear and from that fear created deprivation, loss, disharmony, poverty and struggle.

God does not see the struggle since that is not how He created our lives to be. He created us to live as He lives, in abundance, freedom, love, peace and total joy. Since He gave us His total creative power, we have the power to create either life for ourselves: a life of joy, love and peace or a life of misery and deprivation.

If we view the world as a bad place, we will experience it as a bad place. If we view the world as a place of harmony, cooperation, innocence and abundance, that is also what we will experience. Our beliefs about the world seep out of us in our thoughts, words and emotions. Our actions just follow our beliefs. It is impossible for our beliefs not to come out. They ooze into every thought, feeling, desire, decision and action.

Our thoughts, words, emotions and actions carry our energy out into the world and that energy finds a similar energy and brings it back to us in a physical form. The world acts as a mirror to us, reflecting back to us in our physical lives a form that exactly matches the vibration or the energy of our beliefs.

It doesn't matter if the beliefs are conscious or unconscious, they are energy just the same. We need only look at our physical lives to see the beliefs inside of us. If our physical lives are a reflection of abundance, peace, harmony, love and joy, then our beliefs are based on the reality of what God created. For most of us, our lives don't always reflect those things and that's how we know that there is a belief we need to change.

We have all literally trained our five senses to see, hear, taste, touch and smell according to our beliefs. Take our eyes for example. Our vision is just a picture. It has to involve our mind to interpret the picture. Our mind will interpret the picture only from the vantage point of our beliefs. It has to.

Our mind doesn't interpret anything without running it through a set of filters we call beliefs. It literally filters out anything that isn't congruent. So a false belief that the universe is limited and there's not enough to go around will be filtered by our five senses to "prove" that we are right. All around us all we will see, hear, taste, touch and smell will be limitation and scarcity.

In that way, our false beliefs ensure their existence because they have our five senses trained to testify for them.

Each of us has been socialized to trust only what our five senses tell us. In trusting only our five senses, we are making it very difficult to uproot our false beliefs. But by trusting in the knowledge of what God created instead of our five senses, we will create new beliefs that are based on truth. And from those new beliefs, we will create for ourselves a world filled with love, cooperation, innocence and harmony.

Many of us already suspend our five senses when we think of loved ones that are no longer living on Earth. Many of us believe, in one way or another, that such loved ones still exist, but without having a human body. That belief defies our five senses yet many of us maintain that belief or at least imagine the possibility of that belief being true.

This is an example of suspending our five senses. If we can suspend our five senses in one area, we can also suspend our five senses in other areas. Any area within ourselves that we desire change is a good candidate for suspending our five senses. To suspend our five senses is an exercise in believing in our Godness rather than our five senses.

The use of our imagination is a powerful way to practice accessing our Godness. Imagination itself is an act of suspending our five senses. Our five senses are not needed in our imagination. We can imagine ourselves as having an attribute of God and in doing so our five senses are automatically suspended.

For example, if our pain in life revolves around money, our underlying false beliefs will attract people and circumstances into our life that cause us financial pain. Our physical eyes and circumstances will convince us that the painful situation is real.

But if our desire to live in abundance is strong enough, we can consider imagining ourselves as living abundantly. We can suspend our five senses, by using our imagination, and see only abundance surrounding all of our circumstances. And because of the power of our mind, our finances will begin to change to physically be more in alignment with our natural state of abundance.

Why does all of this bad stuff seem to be happening to us?

There is nothing happening to us. We are simply experiencing what we have created with our false beliefs, thoughts, emotions and decisions.

We focused on our Godness attribute of abundance and our specific desire for financial freedom. We attracted the means to experience a high degree of financial freedom. Then we reached a point where the physicality of our lives exceeded the abundance of our consciousness. This created the circumstance of beginning to lose money.

The losing of money was a stimulus for us to uncover deeper and deeper false beliefs relating to abundance. We became afraid. Our fear opened up deeper layers of fear in our consciousness that related to abundance. This caused us to lose even more money. Our present circumstances are still in flux as we are deciding what we really believe about our Godness and about abundance.

We are the masters of our physical circumstances. We are the masters of our minds. We have designed our present circumstances as a perfect reflection of our consciousness.

How does God see my fellow man?

God sees everyone the same. He sees no difference because to Him we are all Him. When He looks at us, He sees only Himself.

He can't see any of us as separate from Himself since God can't be divided or separated. Therefore, He can't see any of us as separate from each other. If we are not separate from God, then we are not separate from each other.

God sees each of us as innocent and blameless because that is how He created us. He cannot and does not judge us because to Him that would be judging Himself. He sees all the things we call sins as one big mistake in that we think we are separate from Him. That is all. Everything we think of as a sin really started as a thought that we are separate from Him. He wants only to correct our thinking and show us that we are not, and never have been, separate from Him.

If everyone is the same, there is no need for judgment because how can we separate out into categories that which is equal? If there are no real differences, where is the need for judgment? God created each of us with the fullness of Himself and, beyond that, any differences that we imagine that exist between us are illusions based on our belief in our separation from God.

If we are all one with God, then we are also one with each other, and being one, there are no differences that exist between us. And without differences, there is no need for judgment.

The extent to which we see our fellow man as being different from us is the extent to which we will also see God as being different from us. The more we see differences, the less we think we are one with God. How can we possibly be one with God and yet see our fellow man as different?

What exactly is judgment and why do we all seem to be trapped into doing it?

Judgment is placing others in right/wrong/good/bad categories. It stems from a belief that we are separate from God and therefore separate from each other.

Believing that we are separate from each other, we try to make ourselves "better" in our own and God's eyes. We take what we don't like in ourselves and unconsciously project it out onto someone else thinking that this will make it theirs and not ours. This attitude of "it's in you, not me" separates us.

Judgment will always separate.

Then, feeling separate, we can judge the other person as wrong/bad and see ourselves as right/good and we somehow think that makes us better in the eyes of God. If we didn't have it in ourselves in the first place, we would have no frame of reference for judging.

For example, if a Martian came to earth, they would have no frame of reference for fat, pretty, successful, poor, dirty, talented or greedy unless they also had beliefs within them that pertained to these things.

What happens when we judge another person is that we think we are using a yardstick on someone else but not on ourselves. But whatever yardstick or measuring device we use on another person, we will also use that same yardstick on ourselves, either consciously or unconsciously.

For instance, if we are a person who works out and watches what we eat because we think it helps us stay fit and trim, and we judge others for not doing the same, then we will also judge ourselves every time we slip from that standard and blow off a workout or eat a piece of cheesecake.

Our fellow man is a mirror to ourselves.

Whatever we perceive in others, we will perceive in ourselves, consciously or unconsciously. In fact, every time we perceive a trait within another person, we are only strengthening that trait within ourselves.

So if we go around noticing love, joy, patience, kindness, harmlessness, innocence and power within others, we are further connecting with our God energy that has those same traits. The more we notice cruelty, evil, sadness, poverty and weakness in others, the more we are disconnecting ourselves from our natural God energy.

Judgment always says that our way of being is right or good. Judgment says to another person, "I know what's best for you because what's best for you is to be like me." It is only in our feeling of separateness that we need to have others be like us to validate our way of being. It is only in the fear of separation that we crave the security of having others be the same as we are. If others are like us then we feel safer in this world because it means that our way of being is right.

We all believe that there is a right way and a wrong way to live. If we get it right then there will be no judgment from God but if we get it wrong we will be judged by God. We believe the more people that are like us protects us from a judging God. After all, how could so many of us all be wrong?

God doesn't judge and He doesn't see any differences. The fact that we notice differences in others at all is a sign that we have an underlying belief in separation. When we know what oneness feels like, we don't even see any differences, much less try to mold the differences we see to our own version of rightness.

Can I heal my false beliefs alone in meditation or do I need other people to help me heal those beliefs?

All of the people that touch our lives are blessings of God. They serve a huge function to us by being a mirror to us. Everything we see in our fellow man relates to us in some fashion. Because most of us are in such heavy delusion about our unconscious beliefs, we need our fellow man to be a mirror to us.

Our denial of our false beliefs is so strong that without our fellow man, most of us just wouldn't see the falseness of our beliefs. We wouldn't be aware of our mistaken thinking. Even if we were able to see our own false beliefs, we might still have a tendency to defend them instead of change them, much like the way we say, "Well, that's just the way I am."

Every time someone irritates us or we don't like someone or we feel anger towards someone, it is because they are being a mirror for us. They are giving us an opportunity to see within ourselves how our irritation, dislike or anger towards them is really about us.

It is an opportunity for us to see where our false beliefs lie. Behind all negative emotions that we feel towards others is fear that relates to one of our false beliefs. When fear stemming from a false belief is triggered within us, it is an opportunity for us to acknowledge it and then release that false belief.

For example, when we judge another person's mode of driving we might say to ourselves that we are right for waiting in line to turn a corner and our fellow man is selfish for cutting in that line. Our judgment of that person is really all about our own fear.

We fear that we are separate from God and therefore we fear that we can be hurt. When we finally realize that, as God, no one can hurt us and, therefore, however our fellow man behaves is perfect and good, we will finally be able to accept our own behavior and stop judging ourselves and others.

Other people whose behavior bothers us are attracted into our lives to help us see our false beliefs of separation. We cannot release what we don't know about. Our fellow man is here for us so that we can find our way home to living our Godness.

Each moment that we find ourselves in judgment of our fellow man there is an opportunity for us to choose differently and see them as God created them so that we will start to see ourselves that way. As we start to see everyone and everything in our lives as innocent and blameless, we will see ourselves that way as well because they are our mirror in life.

What we see in the mirror is our reality. So, eventually, by seeing others as innocent and blameless, we will be able to let go of self-judgment and our reality will become seeing ourselves as innocent and blameless.

Self-judgment and the thought that we are bad/wrong short circuits our communion with our Godness. We feel unworthy of being and having all that God has given us, which is everything. We will never be able to accept the gift of the fullness of God within us until we see ourselves as innocent and blameless.

Since other people are our mirrors, we must first see it in them before we will see it in ourselves. Any way that we view our fellow man in a manner that is different from the way that God views him is judgment. That judgment of our fellow man is a judgment of ourselves.

How am I to see murderers, poor people or just plain old jerks?

All of us made the same mistake. We all mistakenly thought we were separate from God. A person who murders another does so because he thinks that is what he needs to do to take care of himself. A murder is the culmination of many false beliefs that all stem from the same mistaken belief, that we are separate from God, which is the same mistake we all made. When God looks at a murderer, He sees only that one mistake.

If the murderer knew of his oneness with God, and therefore with everyone, there would never be a cause to attack another person since that would be like attacking oneself. The murder would never happen if the murderer knew he was not separate from God or his fellow man. How could a person want to hurt himself? He wouldn't.

It is only our belief in separation, and therefore judgment, that wants to separate people out in differing categories of sinners. We want to judge others so that we can be at the top of the sin list with just a few little indiscretions and others at the bottom of the list with major life flaws.

We believe in sin and punishment because we believe we are separate from God. God sees no sin. He sees only one mistake that He wants to gently correct. He sees only a misperception in our thinking that He would like to gently wash away and substitute His original thought of our creation.

God doesn't see poverty or evil in anyone because that is not how He created them. He sees only abundance and love. He sees everyone as innocent, blameless and sinless. If we can manage to see our fellow man the way that God sees them, we can then see ourselves that way as well. If we insist on seeing our fellow man as sinful, we will not be able to see ourselves as innocent, blameless and sinless and therefore not worthy of the gift of the fullness of God.

Whatever we see in our fellow man is what we also perceive in ourselves. If we see a person as lacking and in poverty then we will also think it is a possibility for us to live in lack and poverty. However we see other people is the genesis of our beliefs about ourselves. When we encounter a person who is living in poverty instead of abundance, cruelty instead of love, or sickness instead of health, we do them and ourselves a favor if we can manage to see them the way God sees them.

God does not see poverty. He sees only the abundance He gave to His children.

He does not see evil. He sees only the love He created as His children.

For example, when we encounter a homeless person on the street, if we can see them as the abundant, powerful child of God that they are, we give them an opportunity to see themselves that way.

Our thoughts send out energy to the people we encounter and that energy is felt by them at some level. If we agree with a person's belief that they are separate from God and therefore poor or evil, we only increase that energy within them.

But if we can instead see them as powerful, full of love and abundant, we offer them an opportunity to change their thoughts and agree with God. When we disagree with a person's opinion about their poverty, sickness, weakness or safety we weaken those beliefs within them as well. In our society, we are viewed as being uncompassionate and hard-hearted unless we feel sorry for the poor, the weak, the sick and the suffering.

From God's perspective, it is uncompassionate to see our fellow man in any way but the way He created them.

People seem not to see that their opinion of the world is also a confession of character.
—Emerson

If you treat a man as he appears to be, you make him worse than he is. If you treat a man as if he already were what he could potentially be, you make him what he should be.
—Goethe

Every part of our personality that we do not like will become hostile to us.
—Robert Bly

I am in you and you in me, mutual in love divine.
—William Blake

Chapter 5

The Heart of Truth

The search for truth is but the honest searching out of everything that interferes with truth. Truth is. It can neither be lost nor sought nor found. It is there, wherever you are, being with you. Yet it can be recognized or unrecognized.
—A Course in Miracles

We made very little money from trading over an eight month period. Eight months with little to no income was indeed a learning experience for us. We were living off the proceeds from the sale of some land but our money was quickly dwindling. Even with some small minor financial miracles, we started to doubt our beliefs again and we languished in confusion.

We felt like we were going backwards spiritually. For eight

months now, we had meditated for hours on end and we felt like the answers we received were the truth. This doubt and confusion came as a surprise to us. We found ourselves right back in the midst of fear even after we had spent days, even weeks, in love and joy. The only difference was that this time we weren't panicked and afraid; we were just surrounded by doubts and confusion.

We decided to get to the root of all of our fears. We faced what it was we were afraid of. We found the same fears and false beliefs that we had uncovered previously. So we began to question why they were coming back. What was the step we were missing that would help to permanently transform our minds and therefore our physical world?

We discovered that we had to be diligent in watching our thoughts, words, emotions and actions. We found that there was no "goofing off time" or vacation time. We realized that the only way to truly change our lives was to diligently watch our thoughts, emotions, words and actions and let go of the ones that didn't align with our Godness.

We learned that our lack of vigilance allowed habits to form that were based on false beliefs. These habits took us out of consciously watching what we were thinking, feeling and doing and put us on an automatic track with our false beliefs. We became aware of how many habits we had formed in our lives and in so many areas: physical habits, financial habits, emotional habits, communication habits and mental habits.

We realized that we needed discipline to break some of these habits. The technique that finally worked best for us was to institute additional forms of discipline in our physical lives. Whatever form of discipline we chose, we felt would be a daily reminder that we were committed to a spiritual discipline, a discipline that weeded out the false beliefs and invited truth.

We decided to give up something we loved physically and commit to something we resisted. We gave up drinking a glass of wine with dinner and eating sweets afterwards. We also committed to daily exercise. This physical discipline showed our unconscious mind how serious we were about eliminating false beliefs and instituting truth in our lives. It worked. We soon felt confident again in what we were being told in our meditations and we gained the strength to ignore the physical circumstances surrounding our financial condition.

What is fear?

All of creation is made of the energy of God.
That is the truth of creation. There is only truth. Nothing else exists. Love is the emotion of truth. All else is but an illusion of something that is not there. Fear is the emotion of illusion.

All fear relates to the belief that we are separate from God.

If we believed in our oneness with God, there would be no fear.

If we truly knew our oneness with God, what would there be to worry about since God cannot be hurt or diminished?

If we knew our oneness with God, wouldn't everyone and everything work in cooperation and harmony with us?

If we truly understood that we are one with God, would there be anything we couldn't be or have because God is everywhere and is everything?

If we became truly aware of being one with God, could we imagine any hurt, pain or sickness that we would ever need to protect against?

Since we are not and never have been separate from God, all fear is unjustified. There is never one moment that any of us need to spend in any form of fear. Fear has many forms and variations but all fear stems from our insistence on one false belief: that we are separate from God. Sometimes this is a conscious insistence, but more often it is an unconscious insistence. Nonetheless, it is still insistence.

If we focus on our oneness with God,
fear must vanish because there can be no fear
where God is. God is light and there can be no
darkness where one speck of light exists.

We only believe there is darkness because we focus on our fear. When we focus on our Godness, all we see is light.

If we truly believed in the creative power of the Godness within us, there would never be a need for worry or concern. Every moment the Godness within each of us is creating whatever we tell it to. We tell it what to create with our minds, our emotions and our actions. What shows up as our thoughts, emotions, words and actions originates from our deepest beliefs.

Or, in other words, we generally think, feel, speak and act based on our underlying beliefs. We create in our physical world by thinking, feeling, speaking and acting. When we allow thoughts, emotions, words and actions that are based on fear, the creative power within us creates the very things that we are afraid of.

Whatever we worry about, shows up in our lives.

For example, if we have a basic false belief that we are separate from God and that we can therefore experience financial deprivation and lack, it might show up as the fear of running out of money. This belief in the fear of running out of money drives our thinking, feeling, talking and acting regarding our money.

In addition, the vibration of our false belief, the fear of running out of money, goes out into the universe like a messenger looking for a twin vibration to bring back into our physical world. This will show up in our lives as a circumstance or situation that exactly matches what we are afraid of: running out of money.

As we place more and more of our attention on this fear and the emotion of worry, the energy of "I am worried about running out of money" increases and our fear is confirmed with more and more circumstances of financial lack. We end up attracting the very thing we are afraid of, which is running out of money.

It's as if we've been given a giant fire hose of creative power and we don't know how to use it. Most of us use this giant fire hose of power against ourselves by focusing its power on fear. The fire hose of power will create whatever we focus it on.

One way to keep focused on love instead of fear is to live only in the present moment. Fear can only live in the past and the future. Love only lives in the present moment. If we stay focused on the present moment, there is no fear. But the moment we look backwards to the previous moment or forwards to the next moment, we are in fear.

> ***Looking backwards, fear will always tell us that whatever pain we experienced in the past will occur again in the future. Looking forwards, fear imagines all types of painful outcomes based on past experiences.***

Our Godness is with us every moment. We are not separate from it. Our Godness is fully able to take care of any desire or need within every moment. We block the manifestation of our desires by focusing on pain, worry, and fear. Whatever we focus on is what our Godness creates for us. Only if we choose to focus on pain, worry and fear will those things be created.

If we can manage to focus our attention in the present instead of the past or future, we open ourselves up to all kinds of wonderful possibilities. If we let the past creep into our awareness, our possibilities start to get limited by our past experience. Our experience says, "That good thing can not happen because it has never happened before" or "This horrendous thing will happen again because it happened before."

If we focus on the future, since we're not in the unlimited present, we are by definition having to consciously or unconsciously draw upon the past to imagine our future, so again we limit our possibilities.

If we allow our attention to be focused on the past or the future, we dilute the power we have in the now. Creation happens in the now. Now is when all possibilities are open to us. When we stay in the now, we can create unlimitedly.

How can I learn to live in the present?

Realize that life can only be fully lived in the present. There is no life in the past or the future. The past is only a memory and the future is only a projection of the past into the future.

We have trained ourselves to use our past experiences as our guide into the future. We believe that the way we have lived so far is the way to continue living. We store our memories of the past below the surface of our awareness and have trained our memories to present themselves in every instant in the present that relates to a particular memory of the past. Without even realizing it, we are usually drawing upon past memories to guide us into a future that we are worried about in the present.

A memory of the past is only a memory of an experience in the past. Each moment can only be experienced once. Whatever we experienced in the past cannot be experienced exactly the same way again. We can only carry around a memory of the experience.
If we consciously or unconsciously bring a memory of the past into the present moment, we have diluted our ability to fully experience that moment. Since the fullness of God is available for us to experience every moment, bringing memories of the past into the present moment will only short circuit our experience of our Godness.

The future does not yet exist. It is only a projection of our minds. We cannot experience what has not yet happened. We can perceive what we expect the future to be but that is not the same as experiencing. Experience only happens in the present. The future cannot be experienced.

The attention we give to the future is a dilution of our attention to the present. When we think and feel thoughts and emotions about the future, all we are doing is perceiving a mental or emotional projection of something that may or may not happen in the future. We aren't really experiencing anything.

If we allow ourselves to focus on memories from the past or projections of the future, we will never really fully experience the present moment. A part of us will always be somewhere else.

To be fully alive is to fully experience.

If we are living in the past or the future, we are then, in reality, only partially alive.

To be fully alive means that we are singularly focused on the fullness of the present moment.

There is never a reason to bring the past or the future into the present and, if we do, it only serves to block our experience of the present.

Fear can only be present in the past or the future. If we live in the present moment there can be no fear. But the moment we step into a past moment or a future moment we open ourselves up to fear.

By living in the present, with fear removed, all that's left is the fullness of our Godness. We block ourselves from fully experiencing ourselves, our Godness, by shading the present with a memory or perceiving an illusion of the future.

Our Godness is capable of expressing through us the fullness of God every moment. Our Godness knows what we desire even before we consciously know what we desire. That is why the present moment is always completely sufficient unto itself. To live fully present in this moment is to have a full experience of ourself, of our Godness, and the vibrancy of our connection to everyone and everything else in the world.

When we live our lives only in the present moment, with our Godness fully engaged, colors are more intense, tastes are more flavorful, scenes are more beautiful. When we live only in the present moment, we notice textures, colors, shapes, emotions, and sounds. All of our senses are heightened, including our intuition and communion with our Godness.

This heightening of our senses allows us to be more aware and conscious of everything and everyone around us. A side benefit of living in the present moment is that it puts us in a natural state of joy because we are able to "in joy" everything and everyone around us more fully.

How can I recognize fear?

Fear has many disguises. Anger, jealousy, hatred, worry, anxiety, impatience, guilt, confusion, doubt, indifference, cruelty, and distrust are just a few of its costumes. Every emotion that we humans can come up with resonates with either fear or love.

The best way to recognize fear is first to know love. Then we can know what is not love is fear.

Love is clear. It doesn't live in mixed messages.

Love is abundant. It is never constricted in any way.

Love is sharing. Love always believes there is plenty for everyone.

Love is at peace. There is nothing that can disturb it.

Love is certain. It trusts itself.

Love is wise. There is nothing, at some level, love does not know.

Love is attention. There is nothing that passes by it unnoticed.

Love is pure. It is unspoiled by anything that is not of itself.

Love is beautiful. It needs no form to make it so, yet every form it touches transforms into beauty.

Love is whole. It is complete within itself.

Love is unlimited. It cannot be measured because it is infinite.

Love is balanced. It doesn't ask for obligation or sacrifice.

Love is strong. Love knows no weakness and there is nothing stronger than love.

To recognize fear, we can also watch our thoughts, emotions and actions for signs that we are resisting or avoiding fear. If we find that we are resisting or avoiding anyone or anything in our lives, we can know that fear is there.

Sometimes our resistance looks like defensiveness. Love needs no defense. Truth needs no defense. Fear will always need to be defended.

Sometimes avoidance looks like busyness. Love stays peaceful and centered. Only fear hides behind stress and urgency. There are many disguises to fear and we have been equally clever in our patterns for avoiding or resisting it.

Sometimes it is hard to recognize fear thoughts since thoughts are strictly mental. That is why we've been given a gyroscope of sorts that we call emotions. Our emotions are simply the experience of our thoughts, conscious and unconscious.

When we are in fear, our emotions will run the spectrum from being uncomfortable, constricted or confused, to just feeling downright painful. When we are in love and truth, our emotions will feel clear, certain, pleasant, peaceful and expansive.

How do I handle fear?

There are several ways to deal with fear. Many of us simply resist it. We feel the fear inside of us and we defend ourselves against it. Others of us avoid it. We run from fear by busying ourselves with other things. Still others of us feel the fear and deny that it is there. It doesn't matter whether we deny fear exists within us, we avoid it or we fight against it, we get the same results.

Denying that fear exists within us is like fear knocking on our door and we don't answer it. Nothing changes and the fear knocks more loudly. Avoiding fear is like answering the door and quickly slamming it shut again and running away. A part of us knows that fear is there, knocking on the door, but we just avoid listening to that part of ourselves. Nothing changes and the fear knocks more loudly. Resisting fear is like answering the door and throwing a few punches at the fear before we slam the door. The fear only punches back harder and keeps knocking more loudly.

The only way to deal with fear is to embrace it and see it as your best friend. Only a best friend would keep knocking when they are ignored, avoided or resisted. Fear needs to be embraced because fear carries with it a gentle and loving message it wants us to hear. Once we hear that message it will go away.

The message fear wants so badly to tell us is always about that moment when our thinking became mistaken and we created a false belief. When we forgot who we were, we created fear which now, if we will let it, will show us the way back to truth. In the story of Hansel and Gretel, they left breadcrumbs to help them find their way home. If we will embrace our fear, we will see that it is like the breadcrumbs, it is there to show us where we made our mistakes in thinking and lead us back to truth.

Fear is like a bubble that can be popped because it is simply a mistake in our thinking. We think we are separate from God and we therefore think we need to be afraid. It only appears in our lives to gently remind us that we have made a mistake in our thinking.

Fear is not something to be afraid of because all that is needed to eliminate it is to rearrange our thinking. If we make a mistake on a math test, we simply erase the mistake and put the correct answer in. It is the same with our thinking. We let go of what is false and it can then be replaced with truth.

Fear only seems to have power because we resist, avoid or deny it. Whatever we resist, avoid or deny seems to have power over us because by our act of resisting, avoiding or denying we are making it knock louder to get our attention. The louder it knocks, the more power it seems to have. Fear is not something to be struggled with. The less we struggle with it, the less powerful it will seem to us and the more powerful we will feel.

If we are having a hard time embracing fear for whatever reason, and can't seem to understand its message, we can still pop the fear bubble. One way to do that is to allow ourselves a moment to take fear to its extremes. If we think about the absolute worst possible conclusion to whatever we are afraid of, and we feel that fear, we will realize that the fear of what we are afraid of is much worse than the actual experience of it.

On the other hand, if we resist feeling our fear at its deepest level, it will only grow within our minds as being larger and more powerful. Once we realize that the fear of what we are afraid of is much worse than the actual experience of what we are afraid of, fear will lose its hold on us. We can then release it and invite truth to take its place.

The main thing to remember about fear is that we created it. It is like a trail of breadcrumbs that we created so that we may unravel it and find our way back to our original mistake in thinking. This time, instead of the birds eating the breadcrumbs (like in the Hansel and Gretel story), we use the fear to see our way back to truth.

Fear, if allowed to express itself, will only point us towards the direction of our false beliefs. Then, when we see the darkness of those beliefs, we can release them and allow the light of our Godness to replace them.

It is said that when someone tells a lie, it must be shored up by hundreds of lies behind it. Fear needs to be shored up even more so. We all develop intricate ways of shoring up our fear and protecting it from truth.

In essence, fear needs to be kept alive by our feeding and watering of it. We literally give energy to fear and make it grow. Some of the ways we do this are by continuing to focus on our experiences of fear in the past and by spending our time worrying about our fears of the future.

Other ways we feed and water our fear are by talking about it with other people. We constantly bring our fear to others and ask them to agree with us that we are limited, our fellow man is bad/wrong, our circumstances are hopeless and that there are really a lot of things we all need to be afraid of. We go to others and ask them to add their fear energy to ours. This only feeds our fear and theirs.

Fear needs to have constant energy added to it because it is not real. In order for us to keep believing it is real, we have to constantly feed ourselves that lie. Truth, on the other hand, stands alone and needs no other energies to feed it because it is real.

The way out of fear is not through fear.
It is through love. To encounter a stimulus of fear and give it no attention is to cut off the water from its roots. Fear cannot live without being watered with more fear. To encounter a stimulus of fear in one moment, and touch the heart of truth in the next, is how to leave fear behind.

What is doubt?

Most people think that doubt is just an absence of faith. But we all have faith every moment. There is no need to ask for it, we all have it and we have plenty of it.

Think about the faith we have in our daily lives. We have faith when a stoplight turns green that the person driving the opposite direction will stop. If we didn't have that faith, we wouldn't drive through the intersection. We have faith that when we put our money into a vending machine we will receive our chosen food or drink. If we didn't have that faith, we wouldn't put our money in the machine.

Faith is simply acting upon what we already believe is true.

What happens when we release our false beliefs is that we open up to a new path for our minds to run on. But the old path still exists. So we end up with conflicting beliefs. We try to think thoughts of abundance and then all of a sudden thoughts of financial lack intrude. Thoughts of limitation arise. We are conflicted in our beliefs. We have the new belief of abundance and we have the old belief of financial lack.

Doubt is just a gentle reminder that our work with our beliefs is not yet finished. We still have some releasing to do.

Doubt is there to show us that somewhere inside of us we believe we are weak instead of strong. We doubt because we don't think we have the power to change our beliefs or create what we want. As we continue to work with our thoughts, emotions, beliefs, words and actions, release our old ways of thinking and doing things, and allow them to be aligned with the truth of our Godness, our old false beliefs will wither away.

When doubt comes up, we simply need to be willing to see the situation from the vantage point of truth. The truth where doubt is concerned is that we are powerful and strong and we are infinitely capable of creating what we want in this world. When we doubt, we are putting more faith in our small belief in ourselves instead of the truth of the way God created us.

What is confusion?

It generally means that there is a false belief within us that we haven't let go of yet. Perhaps we may even be consciously holding on to it.

Think about a ray of sunshine on a cloudy day. The ray is peeking through the clouds but the clouds are obscuring the sun. The sun represents truth and the clouds represent false beliefs. The ray of truth is barely getting through the clouds so we are trying to mix truth with falseness and it feels to us like confusion.

When this happens, the best question to ask ourselves is "What truth am I not seeing?" or "What false belief is blocking me from seeing the truth?" or "What truth have I not been willing to see?"

Letting go of false beliefs creates within us a vacuum that can then be filled with truth.

The Godness within us will never fail to show us truth if we are willing to see it.

What is projection?

Projection is a defense system that we use to protect ourselves from seeing what we are afraid of. The truth is that we cannot be afraid of anything outside of ourselves unless we first have the root of that fear within us.

When we are in fear we project onto people or things that which we are afraid of within ourselves. In our mind's eye, we think we see the attribute of fear in someone else, or in some situation. We focus on the fear that we see in others as a way of denying that it is in ourselves.

When we are angry with someone, the roots of fear are somewhere inside us and we are really just projecting them upon someone else.

When we feel hurt by someone, it is only the fear within us that resonates with the action that the other person carried out.

Whatever emotion of fear we observe in someone else is really present in us. That emotion comes from a false belief within ourselves that is the opposite of our Godness.

It is painful to carry around beliefs that are the opposite of our Godness. It is painful to feel emotions that are fear-based and the opposite of the pure love within us. As we experience people and situations that relate to an aspect of a false belief of ours, we mentally project onto that person or situation our own false belief. We convince ourselves if another person has a characteristic we don't like, that we don't have it. We judge others to have false beliefs that we actually have.

Because judgment always separates, we separate ourselves from our own false beliefs by judging them. We further separate ourselves by projecting our false beliefs onto someone else and denying their genesis is within us.

This cycle of judgment and projection separates us from ourselves and from our fellow man. We will never learn about the truth of our Godness as long as we stay stuck in the cycle of judgment and projection. By continuing this cycle, we create the pain of not knowing our true selves.

It sounds like there is really nothing to be afraid of. Is that right?

That is correct. To be afraid is to immerse ourselves in the emotion that accompanies the belief that we are separate from God.

Fear is the emotion of illusion.
Love is the emotion of truth.

Apply the emotion of love to any situation and fear will be diminished. We cannot diminish fear with fear. Fear will only breed more fear, which in turn will strengthen the false belief of separation from God. This can become a vicious cycle that can sometimes be difficult to release. Realize that being one with God there is literally nothing to be afraid of. Choose love instead and fear must vanish.

How do I choose love in the face of fear?

Choice is always an act of free will and we are always free to choose love or fear. Fear is seductive and always wants more of itself. We give fear more of itself when we believe it is real. We then fight against it in order to defend ourselves. This is how we keep fear in our lives.

We add fear to fear by believing in it and by defending against it with more fear. The original illusion is the belief that we are separate from God. From this original illusion springs countless other illusions that are all attempts to protect ourselves from the fear produced by the original illusion. All fear perpetuates the original illusion. All defense against fear makes more fear. There is no way out of fear through fear.

We all have fear within our consciousness that is sparked when we experience something that relates to the false belief that the fear is based on. We must begin to realize that fear is a choice. We choose what thoughts we keep, what emotions we pay attention to and what actions we take.

To choose love in the face of fear is not easy and it takes discipline. When the fear seems greater than we are, we can at least choose to be willing to let go of the way we are thinking. In any given situation, we can at least be willing to see it from love's perspective instead of seeing it from the perspective of our false belief. We can exchange the way we see it for the way God sees it.

The fear will remain and continue to grow as long as we choose to hold on to our current false beliefs. But as we choose to let go of our beliefs and their corresponding perspectives, fear will be diminished and love and truth will take up residence in our minds where fear once lived.

Choosing love and truth brings peace. With the peace of truth, we can experience fear and not be afraid of it. That is when fear retreats and love begins to grow.

Give light, and the darkness will disappear of itself.
—Desiderius Erasmus

It is not that you must be free from fear. The moment you try to free yourself from fear, you create a resistance against fear. Resistance, in any form, does not end fear. What is needed, rather than running away or controlling or suppressing or any other resistance, is understanding fear; that means, watch it, learn about it, come directly into contact with it. We are to learn about fear, not how to escape from it, not how to resist it through courage and so on.
—J. Krishnamurti

Anxiety is the gap between the now and the later.
—Fritz Perls

One does not become enlightened by imagining figures of light, but by making the darkness conscious.
—Carl Jung

Come, come, whoever you are,
Wanderer, worshipper, lover of leaving—it doesn't matter,
Ours is not a caravan of despair.
Come, even if you have broken your vow a hundred times
Come, come again, come.

—Rumi

Chapter 6

Our True Nature

We who lived in concentration camps can remember the men who walked through the huts comforting others, giving away their last piece of bread. They may have been few in number, but they offer sufficient proof that everything can be taken away from a man but one thing: the last of the human freedoms—to choose one's attitude in any given set of circumstances, to choose one's own way.
—Viktor Frankl

As the months wore on with little or no income and our monies dwindling, we started taking a look at material possessions in a different way. Our first reaction was to spend nothing. Of course, we had to eat and pay rent but beyond this everything else became a huge spending decision. This felt very constricted and we knew that God was in no way constricted or financially lacking. We also knew that if we continued to live like this we would only attract more lack and constriction in our lives.

It was hard to see our bank account disappearing and not live in a constricted way. We knew that we had to live in accordance with all of our needs and desires being met or else we were limiting our Godness. We knew that we were created with an abundant, prosperous Godness within us and there was no circumstance that would change that. We made a decision to live abundantly, no matter what our bank statement said.

By making a decision to live abundantly, it made us define that for ourselves. We had to decide what was abundant and what was excessive, what was really a desire and what was something material we were using to fill up a perceived lack inside ourselves.

We started looking at the motives behind our current and past spending. We realized that while working in corporate America we quite often spent money on things and experiences that we neither needed nor wanted. We spent money during that time to make ourselves feel better about the fact that we were both working in jobs that we didn't like, jobs that took away our most precious commodity, time. It was a silent deal we unconsciously made with ourselves and each other.

At the end of our questioning, we found a financial balance we call *plentiful simplicity*. We had everything we wanted and needed. None of our friends or family ever knew that we had a financial downturn. We still lived very abundantly. We still took vacations. We still had friends and family over for dinner and even sometimes went out to dinner. We still kept our cell phone. We still treated Barbara's mom to the movies once a month. But we lived with a simplicity that neither of us had ever experienced before.

We found a financial balance, abundant and plentiful, yet simple and not excessive. It was a very beautiful discovery for us. It sounds strange but to us it seemed like the money we were living on stopped flowing out of the bank account so quickly and it seemed instead like our money was multiplying in the bank. It seemed like our money stretched so far and met all of our needs and desires that it felt to us like we had plenty of money. Our rational minds didn't quite think so yet, but that is how it began to feel emotionally to us. We knew that feeling like we had an abundance of money was in alignment with our Godness and that emotional alignment would only serve to improve our finances.

What is abundance?

Most people think abundance means having more than enough. Abundance is not more than enough because God creates perfectly. God creates the perfect amount within the perfect sequence of time. Everything that is created in our lives by our Godness is created perfectly for us. We may judge how much is created as being more or less than enough but the Godness within us knows exactly how to answer every desire in physical form.

Living abundantly is simply allowing the Godness within us to fulfill all of our needs and desires with the perfect form.

That includes more than just material things. Material wealth means nothing if you don't have love, joy, health and fulfillment with it. These are all attributes of God.

True abundance means living in a manner that reflects the true nature of the Godness within us.

What if I want to manifest something specific in my life?

In the beginning, God was everything and everywhere. There was nothing that was not God and nowhere He was not. Therefore, everything that we see in our physical world is made of God's energy, even if it is all an illusion of form, and all of that energy is vibrating.

What distinguishes one thing from another in our world is simply the rate at which the energy in and around it vibrates. Our human eyes have been trained to see the vibrations of colors and textures as different, but their core God energy or substance is the same. Creation is simply moving that energy around. We are not really creating something new because there is nothing that is not God.

Everything we want and need has already been created in its essence, its underlying energy, and it was created out of God just as we were. Everything we want already exists as pure God energy.

What we are doing when we create is using our internal God power to attract back to us the energies that essentially match the energy we are transmitting. We transmit energy every moment with our beliefs, emotions, thoughts, words, and actions.

The essence of every desire within us can be traced back to the very nature of God. We all want love, power, abundance, creativity, beauty, fulfillment, harmony, unlimitedness, safety, health, strength and freedom, just to name a few.

When God created us it was His intention that we have all of these things. That is why He gave us the fullness of His creative power, so that we could create this for ourselves. The Godness within each of us wants only to manifest all of these things for us in our physical world. But the energy that we put out is a composite of three types of energies. This composite is made up of our energy that we are consciously aware of, our energy that we are not consciously aware of and the pure God energy of our beingness.

We attract back to us a physical energy that compliments our composite energy. If we desire a house, we will not attract back to us a boat, unless, of course, we desire to live on a boat. The desire for a house distilled down to its essence might be a desire for security, safety, financial well being, abundance, beauty or creative expression.

The essence of our desires mixed in with our composite energy is always fulfilled by our internal God power. But the essence of our desires may look differently to us than the manifestation we had envisioned. Energy is not literal. It is fluid and virtual. Therefore, what we create with our internal God power will match the essence of our composite energy. It may show up in our lives literally the way we want it to or it may come in a different form or time frame.

John Lennon is quoted as saying, "Life is what happens to you while you're busy making other plans." The "other plans" are the forms that we envision in our minds while the "what happens to you" is the ultimate end result of what our composite energies have attracted to us.

If we wanted a house for creative expression and instead we were supplied with a new job that gave us the challenges and creative expression we were seeking, we might not recognize it as a manifestation. On the other hand, we might visualize a specific house we desired and that manifestation might come exactly as we envisioned it.

When we have a desire, we can become attached to having it manifested in a specific form or we can allow it to spring forth from our Godness with the perfect form of its manifestation.

The energy of attachment to having a specific form is an energy of fear. Underneath our attachment is the belief that we need to have our desire manifested in a certain way or we will have some form of pain in our life.

The energy of unattachment is an energy of love. Underneath an attitude of unattachment is a trust and faith in our Godness.

Attachment may manifest the object of our desire, but it will never be as magnificent as the manifestation of unattachment. When we are attached, our fear is controlling our manifestation. When we are unattached, our Godness is in control.

Unattachment is a direct link to the origin of our desire. Attachment is a limitation we have put on our desire.

It is highly unlikely that any of us would be 100% aware of our energies since what we know about our conscious energies of thought, word and deed is just the tip of an iceberg of unconscious energies. The more we can align mentally, emotionally and with our physical actions to the Godness inside of us, the quicker and easier we will be able to consciously manifest what we want.

Aligning our thoughts, emotions and actions with our core beingness will, over time, change even our most deeply rooted beliefs. As our false beliefs are transformed and we are in alignment with our Godness, physical manifestation occurs.

Total alignment implies pure intention at all levels with no conflict at any level.

Total alignment would mean that we literally think, feel and act in the beingness of God.

Total alignment would mean that we would think only the thoughts that God would think, feel only the feelings that God would feel and act only in ways of love and extension as God would act.

Total alignment would mean that we would stay focused only on being God.

Total alignment would mean that we would instantaneously manifest our desires.

Although many of us have experienced this at different times, most of us are content to play with our energy within the parameters of space and time. God is not confined by space. He is everything and is everywhere. God is not confined by time. He always was and will always be. When we live outside our Godness we create limitations of time and space for ourselves.

Our only limitations are our false beliefs. If we can see our false beliefs as the roots of weeds, and our thoughts, emotions and actions as leaves and stems of those weeds, we can see that the best way to get rid of the weeds is to rip out the roots. However, if we keep stripping away the leaves and stems over time, the roots will also grow weary and die. And if we also plant new roots (truth) right beside the old ones, the new ones will also help to choke out the old roots.

To manifest anything in our lives we first need awareness. We need to know ourselves deeply. We need to find as many false beliefs as we possibly can. We need to know what our desires are. We need to know the Godness within us. We need to watch, like a reporter or a private investigator, the thoughts, emotions, words and actions that we see ourselves thinking, feeling, speaking and doing. We need to align ourselves mentally, emotionally and physically with our Godness. We need to focus on the essence of what we want and trust the Godness within us to create with us using the laws of cause and effect.

We, the totality of our energies, are the cause and the Godness within us is the power to create the effect. We need to understand that our false beliefs are screaming at us to look for change outside of ourselves. But we must change inside first.

Our physical world only changes as we change and it always changes as we change.

Is it okay to have desires or should we just be happy with whatever is manifested?

All of our desires relate back to the attributes of God. Every desire we have can be boiled down to an essence that relates to desiring beauty, power, love, abundance, freedom, peace, unlimitedness, certainty or one of the other attributes of God.

Desire is God's way of helping us to remember who we really are.

When we desire something, we are really just recognizing that the attributes of God are missing from our lives and that they naturally belong there. Having a desire just lets us know that one of the attributes of God is about to be expressed in our lives. Before we even have, or recognize, a desire it is already fulfilled because every desire comes from an attribute of God that we already are and have that was willed by God when He created us.

God desires us to awaken to the remembrance of who we really are. Desire is an awakening to an aspect of our Godness. By desiring our Godness, we are creating the physical manifestations of the attributes of God out in the world. The essence of our desires cannot help but manifest because it relates to what God has already created.

What God created can't be changed or altered. By focusing on the essence of our desires, we are using the same creative intelligence to manifest our desires as God used when He created us.

Desire is the energy of our Godness coming out to express Itself.

What is the difference in having a desire coming from my core beingness and wanting material things to fill up a perceived lack within myself?

Desire is our Divine creative energy seeking expression. It can be warped by our false beliefs. It feels the same to us when we use our Divine creative power to create from energies of love or fear. The only way to tell if we are creating from love or fear is to look at the results. Sometimes what we create from fear will look like fear. It will create pain and misery in our lives and the lives of others. Those are the easy ones to distinguish.

But sometimes when we create from fear it looks like love. One way to tell is that in creating from fear we overdo it. We perceive that lack is possible or we think we are unlovable or some other falsehood surrounding ourselves. One way we try to get rid of the false perception is to counterbalance it in the physical world.

For example, if we have an inner belief in financial lack, a belief there's not enough to go around, or a belief we don't deserve abundance, or any number of other lack beliefs surrounding money, we might try to balance that belief out in our physical world by spending excessively. We might try to fill our lives up with any number of material things that we neither want nor need.

Beliefs rooted in lack will always lead to excess.

By filling our lives up with excess, we therefore "prove" the false perception of lack "wrong" but we don't have to change it. We can still hold on to our belief in lack. This becomes a vicious cycle.

For example, our belief in financial lack makes us feel financially unsafe in this world. The more unsafe we feel, the more we buy to make ourselves feel safer. Buying material things doesn't make us one bit safer. We are already totally safe in this world, but this ritual of collecting things makes us feel better about the fear of financial lack inside of us.

This is one way we trick ourselves into thinking we are aligning with our Godness. We think that by buying lots of things, we are aligning with the abundance of God. God is abundant. He does not see or experience lack in any of its forms. He sees no need for excess or hoarding.

God creates everything He needs and wants every moment. God does not even have a concept of wealth since He is and has everything. To have a concept of wealth, He must have a concept of its opposite, financial lack, and God has no concept of that because God has no opposite.

God lives in the plentitude of His beingness. He does not need to fill Himself up with excess to prove to Himself that He is indeed safe in a world where there can be deprivation and financial lack.

To test for excess, we need to look around us to see if there are things in our lives that we really don't enjoy and use. If we don't enjoy and use it, it is probably excess.

For some people, this may be small things we hold on to like a broken toaster. For others, it may be houses we own that we never seem to get around to visiting.

Some people don't even enjoy their experiences. They travel to Europe only to impress their friends, but the actual experience for them is stressful and not very satisfying.

Anytime we spend money based on our perceptions of what others will think of us, instead of what makes our own heart sing, we are in excess. If we own a Rembrandt and we love it and enjoy looking at it, we are balanced. If we own a Rembrandt because it makes others think we are cultured, we are in excess.

The way to get out of excess is to eliminate our beliefs in lack.

Eliminating our beliefs in lack is the hard part, but we can also take some physical action to outwardly get rid of things surrounding ourselves that we don't need or enjoy. By doing so, we will find a simplicity in our lives that will help us to know ourselves better. If we only had one garment to wear, it wouldn't take us long to decide what it is we like and don't like about that garment. But when we fill our lives with hundreds of garments, we lose our desires in the chaos and the clutter. Simplicity teaches us about ourselves.

Knowing ourselves helps us to manifest what we want in our lives.

God intends that we "in joy" everything in our lives. Most of us think what God wants is for us to say thank you for what we have in our lives. We call that gratitude. But the best gratitude is to be "in joy" over everything and everyone in our lives. That is all God wants. If we can't enjoy something or someone, then we can't be in joy over it either and therefore it is excess.

When you are in excess you can't be "in joy" because your senses are in overload. Think of a kid in a candy store or a child who has hundreds of Christmas presents to open. There are so many things surrounding that child that it becomes very hard for the child to perceive their own desires. What usually happens is that the child starts tearing through the candy store or through their Christmas presents only to get to the next bite or the next present. There is no enjoyment of the present moment. Since there is no enjoyment of the present moment, there is only the memory of the past moment or a projection of the future moment. The child, just like the rest of us who live in excess, has their attention on what just happened or what is about to happen. In either case, there is no real enjoyment going on.

Our joy comes from the experience in the present moment of one of the attributes of God.

This concept of excess stemming from lack can be found in all areas of our lives. We can believe we are unlovable and have a belief in the lack of love and then try to fill that falsehood with an excess of love partners. We can believe there's not enough food or wine to go around and have a belief in the lack of physical necessities and pleasures so we overeat and over drink. We can believe we are not beautiful so we go overboard with cosmetics and plastic surgery. For every area of our lives where we think there is lack, not enough, we try to fill that space with excess.

No one can determine what is excess for another. For one person, it may mean a closet full of shoes. For another person it may mean having one pair of shoes. Excess is a concept we can only determine within our own hearts and minds. It starts with a false belief that we are separate from God which branches out into a belief in some form of lack and results in a convoluted way of tricking ourselves into feeling safer about the lies we have told ourselves.

Why is it important to get rid of excess in our lives?

By getting rid of excess, we uncover our desires that have become cluttered in the excess. By uncovering our desires, we are more easily able to consciously manifest those desires and the joy that comes from experiencing an attribute of God.

The deeper reason for getting rid of excess in our lives is because everything in the universe is balanced. All of nature is balanced, the tides, the seasons and the planets. The natural, and therefore happiest, state of all things living is balance. When things are not balanced, the universe tends to move things toward balance because those entities that are out of balance are in some form of pain.

Since we are literally one with all mankind, when we live in excess someone, somewhere else in the world, will live in lack. When we live in excess, we are literally taking energy that belongs to one of our brothers or sisters.

All material things are energy and when we take in an excess of energy, someone else will live with less energy than they want. We live in an unlimited universe. There is plenty for all of us to have exactly what we want and need but when we take more than we want or need, someone else will live in lack. Both parties will be in pain because they are one and the same.

It is like two people getting a take-out dinner. Each one gets a packet of salt. Because of a mentality of lack, one uses too much salt for his/her tastes. Their food is in excess and they don't enjoy it. The other one does not have enough salt for his/her tastes. Their food is in lack and they don't enjoy it. Neither of them eats their meal in joy. If the one who used too much salt for his/her tastes had given to the one who had not enough salt for his/her tastes, all would be in balance and all would eat in joy.

There is enough for everybody's need but not everybody's greed.
—Gandhi

The superior man loves his soul, the inferior man loves his property.
—Confucius

Joy is not in things; it is in us.
—Charles Wagner

Too many people spend money they haven't earned, to buy things they don't want, to impress people they don't like.
—Will Rogers

CHAPTER 7

AN INSTANT OF TRUTH

*We do not understand that life is paradise,
for it suffices only to wish to understand it, and at once
paradise will appear in front of us in its beauty.*
—Dostoyevsky

We put into action what we were learning about excess. We went through our house and gave away anything that we weren't using or wanting. We had a DVD player that had been sitting in a closet for over a year, still in the original box it had come in and never used. We gave it away. We gave away all of the clothes we had worn in Corporate America. That alone made us feel lighter and less cluttered. We found an abundance we had not found before.

We decided to let our Godness get involved in more of our spending decisions. We stopped being impulsive shoppers and when the desire for something came up, we would let it rattle around with our Godness for a few days and, in almost every case, a better, less expensive version of what we wanted would appear. Sometimes we would even get the item we were wanting for free.

We decided to start an "excess fund." Whenever we wanted something, we noted the price that we would normally pay for it and we would add up the savings from the less expensive but more perfect version. We called that our "excess fund" and we decided to spend that money on other people. It became a game for us. We would shop using coupons and the money we saved we would spend on others. It made coupon shopping a joy. Nothing in the world made us feel as prosperous as giving away money to others.

This made us question whether taking action is more important, or just as important, as changing our beliefs. What we realized is that our actions and our words just followed our beliefs. In other words, if someone believes that they are unattractive, they will walk, talk and act as if no one will ever be attracted to them. But if they believe that they are attractive, they will walk, talk and act that way.

Everyone on earth acts everyday according to his or her underlying beliefs. We can force a different course of action and, over time, we might be able to influence our beliefs. For example, that same person who thinks that he/she is unattractive could force him/herself to go up and ask someone to dance. Over time, this behavior might be able to influence a change in their belief of unattractiveness, but this behavior might also reinforce their belief in their unattractiveness.

In other words, by taking action to walk through our fears even though we are still afraid, we may be able to undermine the fear. But the fear may also undermine us and reinforce itself. It's hard to tell how strongly rooted a fear really is and, if it is deeply rooted and we try to change it by taking action against it, we may just reinforce the fear and make it stronger.

Action, by itself, is not the quickest or best route for changing our lives. We have to change the underlying belief in our minds, then it changes our physical world, our actions, our thoughts, our emotions and our words.

As we began to identify and release our beliefs in lack we were able to take some action like setting up our "excess fund." We also started to see some changes in our financial picture. We were even able to withdraw some money from the brokerage account so that we could start our dream of having permanent, consistent wealth.

We took $10,000 and opened up a CD at our bank and we started getting a check for $55 every month. It certainly wasn't enough to live on but it got our dream started. We also started receiving money from unexpected sources. We received a $2,000 check from the IRS even though we had a very capable accountant do our taxes. We couldn't understand the explanation from the IRS but we were grateful and happy to receive it. We also received a $2,000 check from Barbara's former employer having to do with a clerical error relating to a prior paycheck dating back eight months. We believe that these manifestations directly related to the work we were doing by releasing the thoughts of financial lack within our minds.

Why is the mind so important?

Our minds are the most powerful force on the earth. Nuclear power doesn't hold a candle to the mind of man. God gave us His own mind, which is the most powerful creative tool in the universe.

When God created us, He used His mind to create with. In other words, He thought us into being. Extending Himself fully into us, He gave us everything that He is. Therefore, He gave us the same powerful mind that He used to create us. Each of us has this marvelous, powerful tool.

It is important to realize how powerful our minds are because they never stop their function. Our minds are at work twenty-four hours a day. We are always thinking about, dreaming about or unconsciously storing information about something. Even if we are not aware of it, we are always absorbing and generating thoughts in our minds that consciously or unconsciously become beliefs. Our beliefs, in turn, create our physical world for us.

The mind is so important because it is the tool that has been given to us to create whatever kind of world we want. If we want to change our physical world, we must first change our minds. Whatever we see in our physical world must have been conceived in our mind beforehand. Otherwise, it would not have been made manifest in our physical world. We may not have conceived of the exact form that shows up in our lives, but we have at least believed in the essence of its energy.

Why does it not feel like my mind is powerful?

First of all, we all formed beliefs of being separate from God. These beliefs spawned other warped beliefs about ourselves and God. All of these false beliefs stored unconsciously or consciously in our minds began to create a world that we didn't like. Once we created a world we didn't like, rather than look within ourselves for cause, we looked outside of ourselves to other people, things and God for cause. We not only forgot who we were, but we also forgot about Divine laws of cause and effect.

So we looked outside of ourselves for cause and by doing so we gave up the power of our minds. After all, if we believe that someone or something outside of ourselves can affect our world, then we must also believe that the power must be with them and not us. We all create every moment using our mind, but because we don't want to look at ourselves as the cause of our physical world, we give up our natural God mind power. We do this every time we see something or someone outside of ourselves as "the problem."

Unfortunately, this becomes self-perpetuating. The more we

look to other people and things as the cause of all of our problems, the more powerless we feel. The more powerless we feel, the less we believe in our own Divine mind power and the more we see God, other people and situations as the reason for all of our unhappiness.

In order to use our God-given gift of mind power, we must take full responsibility for creating the lives we currently have and commit to changing our minds in order to change our lives.

How do we form beliefs?

Everything in the world is made up of energy. The things we think are solid mass, scientists now believe are just vibrating energy. The difference between clay and diamonds is the rate at which each of them vibrates. The difference between stone and wax is the rate at which each of them vibrates.

Our bodies and our minds all have a unique vibration of energy. Literally, everything in our physical world is made up of vibrating energy and everything has a unique vibration. Even our thoughts carry with them a certain type of energy. Negative thoughts carry negative, fear-related energy and thoughts of love hold energy that resonates with love.

As we think thoughts over and over, that energy is vibrating in our minds. Repetition and intensity determine which thoughts become beliefs.

If we allow the vibration of a certain thought in our minds enough times it becomes what we call a belief. We don't even have to think about it anymore, that vibration has taken up residency in our minds. This can happen consciously or unconsciously.

The thoughts in our minds are like a path that is walked on in an unspoiled meadow. The first time it is walked on, the grass springs back up right away. After several more times, the grass takes a longer time to spring back. After many, many times of being walked on, the grass no longer springs up. The path has been set and it stays until a new path has been made. That is how we create beliefs with our thoughts.

Sometimes our thoughts create emotions. For example, if we think a friend has stolen a ring from us, we might feel angry, but if we later find out that we misplaced the ring, our anger would be dissipated. The anger we felt came simply from the thought that our friend stole the ring.

In the creation of beliefs, the intensity of our emotions can also determine what is a passing thought and what becomes a bedrock of belief. If we are in a car accident and the fear proceeding impact is fiercely intense, we may create a belief that we will never be safe in a car again. We may not have consciously thought about being unsafe in a car, but the intensity of the emotion we felt may have created the belief.

Why is it important to know what our beliefs are?

Beliefs are simply thoughts that have become automatic. They are the parts of our lives that we rarely question, like the belief in gravity. It is extremely important for us to know what our beliefs are because we think, feel and act according to our beliefs and, as we think, feel and act, we are busy attracting and creating everything in our lives. All of the people and circumstances in our lives have energy that exactly matches our beliefs.

It is also important to know our underlying beliefs because we often go to the state of emotional and mental automaticness. When we get stressed, go too fast, do repetitive actions, drive, or listen to boring material, we zone out. We quit responding to our universe and we go on automatic.

Automatic is simply the state where our beliefs are in charge. Automatic is the opposite of being conscious. What happens when we are in this automatic state is that we automatically create in our physical world the people and circumstances that vibrationally match our beliefs.

If we know what those underlying beliefs are, we have a better chance of catching ourselves in the midst of thinking or acting on a false belief and releasing that energy in the moment to create a result we will be happier with.

How do we change our beliefs?

The reason it seems so hard to let go of our false beliefs is because we have created a false identity to go along with those beliefs. When we release our false beliefs, it sometimes feels like we are letting go of our very selves and this can be scary. Because we feel afraid, sometimes we just struggle against the false beliefs instead of releasing them. This allows us to keep our false beliefs and just stay at war within ourselves: truth versus our false beliefs.

Instead of struggling with false beliefs, we need to simply let them go. Let them pass through us like a bird flying though the air. There is no need to give them attention. In fact, giving attention is the same as focusing.

Focusing is the way our minds add energy to our thoughts, emotions, words, actions and decisions and is, in fact, one of the mechanisms for creating. So we don't want to focus on, or give attention to, our false beliefs because that just adds more energy to them. We simply want to release them. If it seems too hard to release them, we can simply be willing for them to be released and our Godness within will complete the job.

All we need do is be willing to see the truth. Truth is simply the thought of God as He created everything. If we are willing to see the truth, the Godness within us will replace our false thinking and we will remember how natural it is for us to think with God in truth.

The steps that best describe how to change our false beliefs are the following.

1. Allow all of our thoughts, beliefs and emotions to surface within us. If we fight against or suppress anything, we will only add energy to it and it will become larger inside of us.

2. Watch our thoughts, words, emotions and actions for clues to false beliefs within us. Once identified, we can deal with them. Once they are brought into the light, they can no longer hide in the darkness. Once identified, false beliefs are easier to re-identify if they come up again.

3. Releasement is all that is necessary. All we need to do is be willing to see things from God's perspective instead of the false perspective we have formed. By releasing what is not true, we automatically create a space for truth to enter.

What about emotions? Are they important in the creation process?

Emotions are indicators of the thoughts we have been thinking. If we are feeling emotions that feel badly to us, then we have probably been thinking thoughts that are rooted in false beliefs. If we are feeling emotions that feel good to us, then we have probably been thinking thoughts that are rooted in truth.

Many people find it hard to watch what they are thinking and make a determination about whether the thought is rooted in a belief that is false or true. Many people feel that this process leads them to get caught up in mentalness and causes them to get stuck in a cycle of focusing on the false belief. Other people get caught up in trying to fix the false belief with their rational mind.

That's how our emotions come into play. It's easy to watch our emotions and keep focused on things that make us feel good rather than bad. So if we are having a problem with getting caught up in the fear or the false belief within our minds, we can simply do our best to let the thoughts go and just focus on thinking, feeling and acting in a way that brings out emotions that feel good to us.

When we feel ourselves getting pulled toward anxiety, anger, impatience or any other emotion that causes us to feel badly, we simply change whatever it is we are thinking about, or doing, and find something to think about or do, that makes us feel good.

In that way, we are always thinking about truth whether we know it or not. God intends that we spend our entire lives in love and joy and nothing else. And when we are in that state of love and joy, our thoughts are aligned with truth.

After enough repetition, or enough intensity of emotion, a new belief in truth is installed within our minds. When we install enough beliefs in truth, our minds start to resonate in alignment with our Godness and we start to create physically in our world the very essence of God in our lives: abundance, freedom, beauty, safety, harmony, peace and fulfillment.

Over time, emotions can influence thoughts. For example, if we spent a week doing only things that we loved and had no other stimuli, we would probably spend that week in emotions like bliss, joy, love and happiness. Staying for a solid week in those emotions would influence our thinking to be more loving, expansive and creative. So thoughts can influence emotions and emotions can influence thoughts.

Some people find that focusing on their emotions is easier for them than trying to focus on their thoughts. That may be because emotions generally vibrate with more intensity than do thoughts. The more intense the vibration, the easier it is for energy to flow in that direction.

Intensity is a focus of energy and we always get more of what we are focused on. By focusing more on love-based emotions, we create more love-based emotions. Also, the letting go of an intense, fearful emotion creates a void within us which, in turn, allows love to rush in if we continue to remain open and released from fear.

Whether we release emotions that don't feel good to us, or whether we release false beliefs and their corresponding thoughts, doesn't matter. Any path that leads to better and stronger alignment with truth will end in the manifestation in our physical world of abundance, freedom, beauty, safety, harmony, peace and fulfillment.

Sometimes I seem to be dominated by emotions or stuck in them. How can I master emotions instead of being a slave to them?

Emotion is the feeling of thought. Emotion is the energy of

thought that is felt in the body. Without emotion, thought is sterile, cold, non-organic and unconnected. Emotion is the connector of thought with the body, the body with thought.

To live fully human is to experience the organic process of being fully alive. Thought produces emotion. The energy of thought is felt in the body as emotion. To feel emotion is a natural process of being human. To allow ourselves to feel and experience our emotions is part of living fully alive.

Emotions, just like the thoughts or false beliefs that they relate to, are things we get attached to. We think they define us and because of that we give them a lot of our attention. Our attention and attachment to the emotion causes it to grow and to seem more and more powerful to us. The more powerful it gets, the more we resist it in order to get rid of it. The more we resist it, the more powerful it gets. We create a vicious circle, or a cycle, of ever-growing emotion until we finally become exhausted and eventually let it go. The process of becoming exhausted can take hours or it can take years.

Emotions are simply something for us to experience. Emotions are simply a way for us to experience the thoughts within our minds. To experience an emotion is to welcome an emotion. To experience an emotion is to allow ourselves to fully feel an emotion as it is happening.

By allowing an emotion to surface, and to fully feel it, we are experiencing the completion of a thought, belief or impression expressed as emotional energy that correlates with the thought, belief or impression. When something is complete, it is finished, it has no more use or function. It is then easily and naturally released by us without even thinking about it.

When we experience our emotions, we have a sense of being fully alive. We are in tune with what is going on with ourselves by experiencing ourselves in each moment. We feel our thoughts and beliefs moving through us as emotional energy. Our mind is aware of what is going on and what is being experienced and there is a sense of completion to our human experience.

When I have a desire, what is it I need to focus on?

When we have a desire, first of all we must realize that the essence of each desire is directly related to an attribute of God. If we focus on that attribute of God as something that He has but we don't, then we are really focusing on the lack of that attribute. The more we focus on lack in any form, the more we add energy to that lack and we will continue to create lack in our physical lives.

Most of us focus on what we want by focusing on the lack of it in our lives. Sometimes we do this consciously by focusing on our problems. We make our problems the entire focus of our world. We talk about them, think about them and devise elaborate schemes to somehow get rid of them. What we see as a problem is always a manifestation of fear. Love has no problems. It knows that the solution is already within the problem. Fear only sees the problem. The fear of a problem is fearful attention on the problem. It is an energy of entertaining the problem. The fearful attention on a problem says to the problem, "please come."

Sometimes we unconsciously focus on the lack of something in our lives by focusing on what we want. We do this just by the very act of wanting or longing for something. If we long for something, we are constantly telling ourselves that we don't already have it and therefore we are focusing on the lack of having it.

Longing for, or wanting, also carries with it an energy of not being able to have it, not having the power to get it. If we knew we had the power to get it, we wouldn't have to long for it or want it. We would know that we already are it in the larger energy sense and that its manifestation was just a matter of moving energy around with our intention.

That is how God creates. He simply thinks of what He already is and has in a different way. He is and has all energy that exists. He moves it into manifestation with His intention. There is nothing in His heart but love and joy when He creates. He brings His will into the picture by deciding that He will experience Himself in that different way. That is all.

When we create anything in our lives consciously, we need to use God as our template. The creative process is easy and enjoyable.

We must first know that whatever attribute of God our desire relates to, we already are and have that.

And we can feel the emotions that come from being and having that attribute of God.

Then we can think about our physical lives as already being and having that attribute of God expressed within them.

And we can feel the emotions that come from already having that attribute of God expressed in our lives.

Lastly, we can decide to receive and experience the expression of that attribute of God in our physical lives.

Then we can let it go and allow the Godness within us to bring the new expression to our awareness in the physical world.

In answer to the question about focus, there is really only one thing in life to focus on: the attributes of God which we already are and have. God gave us His fullness so there is nothing He is that we are not.

The spirit of God is formless and therefore is everywhere and is everything. To God, there is no difference in being and having. To Him, if He is everything and He is everywhere, then He also has everything.

Each one of us is that same energy and therefore we are everywhere and everything. So anything that we think we want, we already are that, and therefore, we already have it.

Our focus just needs to stay on the attributes of God and the many forms these attributes can joyfully take in our lives, and nothing else.

That is all there is to creating what we want in our lives.

What about action? Don't I need to do anything?

As was stated before, sometimes taking action, even against a fear, will only serve to reinforce the fear. When it is time for us to take some sort of action, we will know. It will be clear and it will feel right. It will feel like it can be no other way.

If there is an unrelenting desire to do something, then the thing to do is to do something on a small scale in the direction of the desire. The action to take is to do something that will remind us of the attribute of God that we already are and have that relates to our desire.

For example, if the desire is to retire from work but the finances aren't in place yet and that desire has been traced down to the attributes of abundance and freedom, a small symbol of freedom or abundance might be placed within the home. If finances allow, a part of the dream might be started such as buying a piece of land that would later be used for retirement. Every time the symbol is passed in the home or the land is visited, it will consciously and unconsciously be a reminder of the attributes of freedom and abundance.

Clarity needs to precede action. Unfortunately, the only clarity we have is often a certainty that we no longer want whatever pain we have been experiencing. At that point, if we can just release the resistance we have been having to whatever pain we've been in, we can start on a new road of clarity.

With the releasement of the resistance, we open a space within ourselves that is now free to be filled with something new. It is at this point that some new shift in our physical circumstances takes place and it becomes obvious to us what to do. Or a shift in our thinking takes place, like a new idea. This is the time to take action, to allow and follow the new path that has opened up.

Too often we try to change things while we are still in resistance to the pain. This is when we try to make things happen and we usually end up making things worse.

Resistance is always about an energy that is focused on what we don't want.

We can't have what we don't want and what we do want at the same time. Our energies are conflicted. By trying to focus on what we want through aggressive action, we usually strengthen the fear inside of us and attract what we don't want.

What about inaction? I feel sometimes like I am stuck in inaction.

Sometimes we get frozen into inaction by trying to live the truth of our Godness only in our minds. This occurs when we just intellectualize the truth. We encapsulate truth as an intellectual construct, all the while holding on to our false beliefs. We can then delude ourselves into thinking that we are changing our false beliefs because we "know" the truth about who we really are. We end up with a sense of intellectually "knowing" who we really are coupled with an intense fear of actually living in the truth of that. Our intellectualizing of truth produces rational excuses of why we shouldn't move in the direction of truth.

Getting caught up in intellectualizing the truth is just another way our ego has devised to keep us mired in our false beliefs. When we recognize that this may be the way we are living, the first thing to do would be to ask ourselves, "What truth am I most afraid of?" and "What false belief do I see the affects of most often in my life?" If we are vigilant in watching our lives, we can uncover the false beliefs and then release them.

As we release more and more of our false beliefs, and our perspective is automatically changed to a certainty of who we really are, we can then proceed with an action whereby we are trusting in our Godness in that moment.

By releasing the fear and allowing the truth to enter our hearts and minds, we are given a quiet certainty that we can then act upon. The experience of walking in truth into the face of fear can be a very powerful one. But if we attempt to take an action that scares us while we are still in doubt about who we are, the action will only serve to increase the fear.

A walk of faith into an experience of truth can open the heart and allow love to flow.

A walk of doubt can never experience truth and will only serve to increase the fear.

What if we have created with our minds a mental structure of fear based on years of worrying that we will get sick or die impoverished?

That is, in fact, what every human being has done in one form or another. We all have the same delusion that we are something that we are not. We believe we are limited human beings when actually we are unlimited God energy living in a human body.

When you get down to it, there is only one way to heal anything and that is to release your false perspective of who you are and allow yourself instead to be in alignment with the truth of your God energy. The truth of your Godness can heal anything.

So if we are worried about getting sick or being poor, we are not agreeing with the truth of our God energy. We are living with the false belief that we can get sick or be poor.

The truth is that we can never get sick or be poor. God cannot be sick and He can't be poor. We can, however, make our bodies appear sick by allowing the false belief that we are separate from God to smolder deep down inside of us.

We can make our bodies appear sick by using the energy of fear, created by our belief in separation, to create one worry after another until we bombard our bodies into a state that looks to us like sickness. We can worry about money, or not having enough money, until we cause ourselves to feel like there is a limited amount.

We don't need to worry about a lifetime of worrying because, in an instant, the truth of who we are can heal everything in our lives. As we align our thoughts, beliefs, emotions and actions with our God energy, we can heal any perceived lack in our lives. Our perceived lack of health can be healed over time or in an instant. Our perceived lack of money can be healed over time or in an instant.

An instant of truth can wipe out a lifetime of worry.

All truly wise thoughts have been thought already thousands of times; but to make them truly ours we must think them over again honestly, till they take root in our personal experience.

—Goethe

The transmigration of life takes place in one's mind. Let one therefore keep the mind pure, for what a man thinks, that he becomes.

—The Upanishads

Any idea seriously entertained tends to bring about the realization of itself.

—Joseph Chilton Pearce

For one who has conquered the mind,
The mind is the best of friends,
But for one who has failed to do so,
His very mind will be the greatest enemy.

—Bhagavad Gita

Chapter 8

The Miracle

Do not struggle. Go with the flow of things and you will find yourself at one with the mysterious unity of the universe.
—Chuang Tzu

Back in High School, Barbara was a cheerleader. In fact, she was Head Cheerleader. Before going to college, she practiced for months at her cheering skills and her gymnastics. She even persuaded one of the male cheerleaders at the college she was to attend to help her get prepared for tryouts. When tryouts came, Barbara was nervous but she was used to performing. When she stepped out to do her cheer, to her amazement, her body wouldn't work. As hard as she tried, she couldn't make her hands clap together or even slap her side. It was as if she was a marionette and someone else was pulling the strings.

Horrific as this incident seemed at the time, Barbara was able to see how she attracted this situation with her fear and false beliefs. But she was also able to see the beauty of it later in life. Having not been chosen as a cheerleader, Barbara turned to a more spiritual path during her college years and she values the growth she experienced there immensely.

Our efforts in the stock market reminded us of the cheerleader incident that Barbara experienced. We poured an enormous amount of energy into making money in the stock market and for a few days it would seem as though we were moving forward a couple of steps in that direction. Then everything would turn around and it seemed as though we were forced to take three steps backwards.

The odd thing was that there was money in the market to be made. We just weren't making it. Whatever trade we were in, it seemed like the market went the other way. Sometimes, the market would go in the right direction but the particular stock we were in would go in the opposite direction. Of course we knew that our fear and false beliefs were attracting this situation, but we also decided that the Godness inside of us would work it out for our good, just like the cheerleader incident.

We began to believe that the God energy within us was gently guiding us toward a new direction. At the same time, we kept focusing on the truth of our natural abundance, not knowing where it was to come from and trusting that if it didn't come from the path we were on, the stock market, then it would come from somewhere else.

All of us have at some time in our lives experienced a feeling or a sensation that our God energy was silently guiding us towards a better outcome than the one we consciously conjured up in our minds. That's where trust comes in.

In our humanness, when we see pain or disappointment brewing, we try to control the situation and avoid anything we perceive as painful. We resist the pain in so many ways until finally we surrender and we find that all along everything in our lives has been working in synchronicity towards the best outcome for us. By resisting the pain, all we've done is prolonged the pain or made it worse.

All along, our Godness has gone before us and paved a better road than the one we imagined. This is what we finally learned from our experiences.

We learned to trust the Godness within us.

We learned that by trusting, life became a beautiful, sacred adventure.

We realized that by being one with God, there was nothing to be afraid of.

We learned to love the surprises in life, unlabeled, unjudged as good or bad, because underneath it all our Godness was always present and working only for our highest good.

We also learned to pay attention to the signposts and the guidance that was there along the way so that we didn't need to attract the really painful lessons.

After about 10 months of continual losses in the stock market, Barbara realized that she no longer wanted to spend her time on that path. She decided that she wanted to go back into the corporate world. She felt that, with the things she had learned over those past 10 months, she might be able to make a difference in the lives that she would touch there. Only this time she wanted to attract a kinder, gentler corporate situation to herself.

The very next day, after she made that decision, she got a call from a recruiter which led to her taking a position at a wonderfully supportive company. However, four months into the job, she realized that she didn't like the amount of travel involved with the job. Within a week, another recruiter called and she moved on to a non-traveling position at a company where there was a high degree of respect for each individual and their personal life.

At first it was scary to go back into the corporate world where she had experienced such intense, overwhelming and harsh situations. But Barbara, being led by her desires, had learned to trust her Godness. Although she didn't know exactly where she was going, she trusted that her Godness was always present and working only for her highest good. What she found was a corporate situation where she could give and receive love. No one there called it that but that was what it was. She also found that as long as she didn't resist anything, her experiences in corporate America were no longer painful.

What is pain and how do I get out of it?

Pain is resistance. All pain is caused by our resistance to the experience we are presently in. Pain can be physical, emotional, or mental, or it can be all three.

Physical pain involves a direct injury to our body or a state of varying degrees of disharmony within our bodies. When we resist physical pain, our perception of it becomes larger than what it would actually be if we did not resist.

Our perception of pain is like a separate entity that we've created that surrounds and encases the actual physical sensation that the body is experiencing. We create acute degrees of physical pain for ourselves that would be far less painful if the fear involved in the perception of pain was not present.

If we allowed the experience of whatever physical sensation we were experiencing, instead of resisting and being afraid of it, our awareness of the experience would open and soften around it. We would feel bodily sensations that were different, but they would not be intolerable. Our body, mind and emotions are all designed to be flexible and fluid and can easily take in and release all kinds of experiences without being devastated. We do the devastating to ourselves.

Emotional pain is caused when we resist the feeling of our emotions. The emotions are there, but if they are not fully felt and experienced they will be stuck in the body and cause emotional pain.

Many people have had the experience of feeling anxious, sad, angry or depressed and not known why. That is because they are carrying around emotions from past experiences. These emotions will eventually come out in the form of an outburst of emotion, recurring anxious feelings or in some form of physical sickness or disease.

Emotions themselves are not painful. It is our resistance to them that causes the pain. If an emotion is allowed to be fully felt it will have completed the experience of the thought, belief, or impression behind it and it will be naturally, and painlessly, released from the body.

Mental pain is caused by fighting with our mind. There are as many ways to do this as there are people, but they all involve resisting whatever is going on in our minds.

When we ruminate, or worry, or obsess over things, we are dealing in the energy of fear. When we do this, we are not keeping our thoughts within the present moment because fear can only exist in the past or the future. Usually this means that we are trying to relive the past or control the future.

We generally do this because we are in resistance to the way things are in the present moment. As we resist the present moment and fight within our own minds, we create mental pain for ourselves.

Sometimes it seems like our minds are running completely out of control. The human tendency is to resist our minds when they are racing by trying to stop the racing or worrying about the racing. If we take a moment to get ourselves centered back into the present moment, we will find that there is no pain or fear in the present moment and our minds will quiet themselves on their own accord.

There is another kind of pain that is even deeper than what has been described. It is the pain of feeling separate from our Source. It is the pain of feeling separate from God. This pain is also from resistance. It is the pain of resisting the truth of who and what we really are. This is the real pain.

Our denial of ourselves is a vicious cycle that grows bigger and bigger as we bury ourselves more and more in the delusions of the world. Over time, our pain gets so great that eventually we begin to let go and allow various aspects of truth to enter our consciousness.

We basically have two battles going on within one war.

One battle is with the physical world and all the many protective devices we've created around ourselves to protect us from the pain of the world.

The other battle is the inner one of continually resisting and denying who we really are.

We are at war with ourselves and we must let go of the battle of trying to protect ourselves in a world that we perceive as painful. Our attachment to pain has to become less important than the willingness to see things differently.

We cannot successfully fight two battles at one time. We always end up giving allegiance to one or the other. Most of us believe that the illusions of the world are real so we give our allegiance to the world, our perceptions and our five senses. We fight against the world to protect ourselves from it and in doing so we give our power to the illusions of the world. Illusions become powerful to us and we believe we have to fight against this power.

There can be no allegiance to truth when we are constantly involved in a battle against ourselves and the world. When we finally quit resisting the experiences of life and open to the truth about ourselves, we can then focus on the final battlefield. On this battlefield, we will discover that there is really no battle, or war, at all. It was only our resistance to truth that caused us so much pain. Once we are open to truth, to living the truth of our Godness, our fear will subside and we will learn to live the love that we really are.

Must I create pain in my life to learn from?

We created pain for ourselves when we forgot that we were one with God. All of our pain comes from the mistaken belief that we are separate from God. From this original belief that we are separate from God, we therefore think that we can be hurt, or impoverished, or limited.

We create pain for ourselves and then our Godness uses that pain to gently turn us back to the truth of our heritage. Given enough pain, everyone will finally surrender their fear and accept the love of God, the oneness with God that has been waiting for them all along.

God never wanted or willed pain for us. He willed just the opposite: joy, happiness, abundance, freedom and peace. We created the pain for ourselves with our belief in separateness. Since we insist that the pain is real, the Godness within us will use whatever we have created in our lives for our highest good. If we create joy in our lives, then He will gently lead us back to our true heritage with lessons of joy. If we instead create pain in our lives, and believe in its reality, our God energy will simply use that pain to gently draw us back into the remembrance of our true heritage as a creation of God.

How can I learn to trust the spirit of God within me?

Every moment, within each of us, the energy of God is at work, loving each of us, teaching each of us, guiding each of us and offering to us the fullness of God. Sometimes we tune into the fullness of God within us. Sometimes we don't.

Many athletes, executives, and mothers have experienced moments of feeling the depths of their power, their love, their wisdom or their unlimitedness.

Many athletes have reported feeling like they are in the zone where they can do no wrong and every move they make is literally perfect.

Many executives know what it is like to be so absorbed and flowing as they make a presentation that their presentation is literally flawless.

Many mothers can relate tales of a moment when they have shared an unspeakable, sacred form of unconditional love for their children.

This Godness within each of us is there and accessible to us, every moment, but it is often drowned out by the drama of life all around us.

When we go too fast, when we do repetitive actions, when we are stressed or when we just simply aren't paying attention, we tend to go on automatic. Going on automatic means our underlying beliefs are running our lives.

Our underlying beliefs have at their center the false belief that we are separate from God. Having that belief short circuits our communion with our Godness. But when we get still, really still, like we do in deep prayer or meditation, we often will hear or feel or experience our Godness.

When we are focused completely on the present moment, which takes us out of fear because fear only exists in the past or the future, we are oftentimes able to hear or feel or experience our Godness. As we align our thoughts, emotions, actions and decisions with truth, it becomes easier and easier to commune with our Godness.

Most of us live in such a way that our communion with our Godness is like a badly tuned radio. We experience moments of deep, close, clear communication and also a lot of static.

In order to learn to trust the Godness within us, we must first commune with the Godness within us and learn who we really are. As we learn to commune with the Godness within us, we will find an energy that is so loving, so gentle, so compassionate, so powerful and so wise.

We will also find that the energy of God within us is constantly at work for our highest good. After we have communed over time with our Godness, and we have experienced our Godness working in our lives, we will learn to trust the spirit of God within us completely.

No matter what situation or circumstance we face, we can turn to the Godness within us and ask for a new perspective. Armed with the perspective of God, there is no situation or circumstance that cannot be healed. Once our mistaken thinking is replaced by God's perspective, a miraculous shift takes place in our minds and a healing takes place in our lives. Everything God has willed for us has already been given to us.

Therefore, the only place that "a miracle" really takes place is in our own minds.

The healing of our minds must precede the physical manifestation and always precedes the physical manifestation. The physical manifestation is automatic and comes from the shift of the energy in our minds.

What about control? Do I need to let go completely?

Control is always about fear. We want to control everything in our lives because at some level we believe we are separate from God. The emotion of separateness from God is fear. This fear permeates everything in our lives and can show up as anything from terror to control.

Control comes from the perception that we are separate from God and we are therefore vulnerable and need to protect ourselves from outcomes we don't like. We want to control everything in our lives because we don't trust that we have the power to create what we want and we don't trust our Godness to create with us the perfect expression of our God energy in our lives.

God does not control. God doesn't plan what will happen in the next moment or look to the past for clues about how to act in the present. God lives fully in each moment, trusting in the fullness of Himself to be sufficient for every moment.

Our wanting to control is about not trusting ourselves to be sufficient in every moment. Our wanting control is about not trusting the Godness within us. Our wanting control ultimately is about our feeling separate from God.

There is never a need to plan, set up, manipulate or control ourselves, other people or circumstances. Each of us is sufficient and complete within each moment to handle whatever arises within each moment. Each of us has access to the fullness of God each moment.

The only way we can ever experience the freedom with which we were created is to let go of manipulation and control and trust our Godness to create a perfect match in physical form to our thoughts, emotions, beliefs and decisions.

Control usually relates to an attachment to a particular physical form. We prefer and become attached to a particular form as opposed to another one. Once we are convinced that we have the power to create and that the Godness within us is constantly guiding us towards the best outcome, we can let go of form and leave the perfect expression to our Godness.

This makes it easier to manifest the essence of what we want. The more attached to form we get, the more it hurts our belief and trust in the process. Attachment is fear based and demands control. Unattachment is love based and allows the perfect form or expression to unfold.

For example, if a person wants more love in their lives and they are attached to having that love come from a particular person, then if that person doesn't seem to respond, it hurts their belief that they have the power to create what they want. We must believe in our own power first.

Secondly, we must believe in what God has already created and willed for us. Then, all that is necessary is to allow the flow of Godness through us into a perfect manifestation of God's will.

Whatever we desire is automatically made manifest because what we desire is the only thing we ever were.

When we try to control the manifestations or forms in our lives, we are limiting ourselves and the Godness within us. We are honoring the ego's temper tantrum which says, "I want this circumstance or situation to be different than it is," instead of saying, "I want to experience the perfect expression of my Godness in this area."

Willingness to receive must also precede the manifestation. We must be willing to receive what God has already willed for us. The trouble is that most of us run up against false beliefs of unworthiness when we think about all that God has willed for us to receive.

Our thoughts of unworthiness are nothing more than our arrogant opinion of who we are which is meant to replace His opinion of us. This substitution of our opinion of ourselves for God's opinion of us is a choice. By clinging to our thoughts of smallness, unworthiness and guilt, we are saying that our opinion is more correct or better than God's opinion of us.

The Miracle

No snowflake ever falls in the wrong place.

—Zen saying

If there is a sin against life, it consists perhaps not so much in despairing of life, as in hoping for another life and in eluding the implacable grandeur of this life.

—Albert Camus

Most of the shadows of this life are caused by standing in one's own sunshine.

—Emerson

If you follow your bliss, you put yourself on a kind of a track that has been there the whole while, waiting for you, and the life you ought to be living is the one you are living.

—Joseph Campbell

Chapter 9

A Powerful Way of Life

*Prayer is the contemplation of the facts of life
from the highest point of view.*
—Emerson

From the moment our financial crisis first hit until the present, we not only meditated daily but we also spent time in prayer. As time went by and we were able to release more and more fear, and as our certainty of our oneness with God grew, we noticed a progression in the way we prayed.

In the beginning of our financial challenges, we were simply begging an outside God for help in resolving this crisis. It was mostly prayers that went something like this, "God, please don't let us get a margin call" or "God, please give us a financial miracle that will restore all the money we have lost."

These sessions were interspersed with "whine sessions" where we bemoaned our fate to God. But as we released our fears and our beliefs changed and we became certain of the absence of separation between God and ourselves, our prayers changed automatically.

We noticed that we seldom asked for anything in a tone of supplication. We realized that only when we were focused on fear did we resort to prayers of asking or supplication.

We watched ourselves as different kinds of prayer poured forth from us. It wasn't something we did consciously. It was something that happened within us as the beliefs within us changed.

We became very curious as we watched this progression. We decided to start asking questions relating to prayer in our meditations. Some questions were very basic and others were more complex, but the answers we received seemed to match the experiences we were having. We are certainly not trying to say that there is a right or wrong way to pray. We believe that all prayer is a sacred and holy outpouring of the human heart.

What is the difference between prayer and meditation?

Meditation is a stilling of the mind. It is a space where thoughts flow without restriction until there are no more thoughts. This space where there is a void of mental chatter allows us to hear the voice of our Godness.

The voice of our Godness comes to people in many different ways. Some people see pictures in their minds, others hear a still small voice within them and others simply have a sense of what their Godness is telling them.

Many people have techniques that work for them to create this space of stillness within them. Some people use breathing techniques while others chant or concentrate their mind on a mantra or a non-thought.

Other people meditate without even knowing that is what they are doing. Many people report that physical exercise like jogging creates this space within them. Other people say that staring at a beautiful painting or beautiful natural scenery creates this space for them. Still others reach the stillness by listening to music.

Some people have mastered the stilling of their minds to the point of literally staying in a waking meditation throughout their entire day.

Some people ask questions at the beginning of their meditations and in the stillness they listen for the answers. Other people take a word or an attribute of God and focus only on that in the stillness. Some people just go to the stillness and allow the voice of God to speak to them without an agenda.

There is no right or wrong way to meditate.

Meditation is important because the drama of our daily lives, and the thoughts and emotions stemming from our false beliefs, drum so loudly within us that it is only in the stillness that we are able to hear the voice of God within us.

When we go for periods of time without hearing the voice of God within us, it only reinforces our false belief of separateness. The more we meditate, the more we know what the voice of God within us sounds like and the less chance we have of being confused by the voice of fear.

To most people, prayer is somewhat different than meditation. To others, the lines of distinction blur. To most people, prayer is an emptying of our hearts out to the Godness within us. It focuses our energy on what it is we desire. By focusing on our desires in prayer, it allows us to get clear about what it is we would like to see created in our physical world.

Prayer is a clarification and prioritization of our desires. The things we pray about are the things that are most important to us. The things we pray about are the things that touch our hearts most deeply. By clarifying and establishing the priority of our desires, our energy is more clearly focused and therefore it gives clear and focused direction to the God energy within us.

Each of us has the power to create literally anything we want to create. That power was given to us by God when He gave us the fullness of Himself. Each one of us is creating with that power every moment.

What prayer does is focus our energy on what is most significant to us so that we more clearly direct this Divine creative power within us.

When God creates, He doesn't need to pray. He is already focused. There is not one variance within the thought of God. When God creates with His thought, there is no other thought to oppose it. When God decides to create with His thought, because it is pure, focused energy, it manifests.

As humans, we have believed the lie that we are separate from God and therefore our minds are split. Our minds are split between truth and false beliefs. When we focus on a thought, there are often a variety of thoughts within us that oppose that thought. So when we try to use our Divine creative powers, we are often sending out conflicting energy.

Prayer helps us to clarify and prioritize the energy of our thoughts and desires so that we are sending out a focused and non-conflicting energy.

When our energy is purely focused, we begin to create in our physical world the way God creates. When our energy is purely focused, we use the creative power given to us by God to manifest what it is that we desire.

To most people, prayer and meditation are somewhat different but sometimes our energy flows back and forth between the two like a pleasant two-way conversation. Other times, meditation remains separate from prayer. Sometimes it's difficult to separate out what is one and what is another. Both are words that we have created to describe our communion with our Godness. Sometimes, it's difficult to describe that communion and since that communion is so sacred and personal, it's best to stay away from labels.

Are prayers answered?

All prayer is right and good because it helps us to better direct the Divine creative energy within us. All prayer is answered in the physical, although we often don't recognize the answer.

One reason we don't recognize the answer is because we get attached to having our prayers answered in a certain way. We get attached to having a certain physical form show up in our physical lives. Attachment to form hurts our believability. We have trouble believing in our creative powers when we get attached to very specific forms. For example, if we focus on having a specific person marry us, rather than focusing on experiencing love, we may have trouble believing that we can create that.

We give energy to whatever we believe in.

So by believing in our divine creative powers, we energize them and it makes it easier for us to create what we want.

Another reason that we don't recognize the answer to our prayers is because we often send out conflicting energy. Through our prayer we get really clear about what it is that we are wanting but we also are sending out the energy of our false beliefs so the answer to our prayer then becomes distorted by those false beliefs.

On the one hand, we are directing our God energy towards creating what we are wanting and on the other hand our false beliefs are directing that same energy towards an opposite form. The result can be a form, or forms, that we don't even recognize but is nevertheless the result of our prayer and the conflicted focus of our energy.

The essence of all desire relates back to the attributes of God. No matter what it is that we desire, it is there within us to draw us toward the expression of our natural freedom, love, abundance, health, safety, certainty, beauty, power, peace and fulfillment.

Even if we look at an extreme example of someone desiring to hurt another person, that desire is there within them to show them the distinction between what they think they are wanting and what they are really wanting.

For example, wanting to hurt another person could really be about wanting to experience the unconditional love of God within us. The pain a person might experience from not feeling loved, or not feeling lovable, coming from a sense of separateness, could be turned into anger or even rage. The rage could be so overwhelming and so painful that it comes out as a desire to hurt another person, to transfer the pain onto someone else.

The true essence of what that person would be wanting is to experience love, which relates back to an attribute of God. Sometimes, our desires lead us first to something we don't really want in order for us to see what it is we truly do want. Over time, even the person who wants to hurt another person will eventually see what it is they are truly wanting.

Sometimes we need the distinction of experiencing what we don't want in order for us to understand what it is we truly are wanting.

Is there a right way to pray?

The way we pray stems from our beliefs. If we believe we are separate from God, then our prayers will reflect that.

One common way to pray is to simply ask for what we want. An example would be, "God please give me this or God please let this happen." This reflects that we believe we are separate from God and that God who is outside of us will answer us.

If we truly believe that we are one with God, there is no need to ask God to give us anything since He has already given us everything He is and has.

By asking a God who we see as separate for help, we are seeing ourselves as powerless. This belief in our powerlessness dilutes our natural creative power and creates results in our lives that reflect this powerless feeling.

However, this type of prayer still focuses our energy on what we want, which purifies and strengthens our energy and that is why this type of prayer is often answered exactly as it is asked.

As we lose some of our fear and belief in separation, our prayers change as well. Sometimes we pray using commands because we have gained some knowledge about our Divine creative power. An example would be, "I command that such and such happen according to God's laws of cause and effect."

Unless we are totally devoid of fear and false beliefs, this type of prayer usually ends in frustration because, deep inside, the reason we are using commands is because we really don't think we have the power to carry this off. We are using commands because we don't feel powerful. We have conflicting beliefs about ourselves, our oneness with God and our powers of creation.

This type of prayer will still be answered because again it focuses our energy on what it is that we want but the answer may be distorted by our false beliefs.

Even though the kinds of prayers mentioned above focus us on what we want, which clarifies and prioritizes our desires, as we believe in our oneness with God we start to let go of any energy of wanting in our prayers. The energy of wanting is an energy of not already having. As we believe in our oneness with God, we realize that we already are and have everything. There is no need for wanting.

Our prayers then become more of an alignment with who we know ourselves to be. Our prayers become more like an experience of feeling what it is like to be God. We start to experience in prayer what it is like to be pure love and nothing else. We start to feel what it feels like to have all of the abundance of the universe. We begin to experience a divine peace that reacts to nothing.

In prayer, we can experience what it is like to be one with everyone and everything in the universe. We can feel what it is like to not know where we leave off and everything else begins. We can experience what it feels like to be at one with the heart and mind of God.

Our prayers, then, become a literal experience of who we really are.

The more immersed we are in our oneness with God, the more our faith is strengthened in the belief that all freedom, love, abundance, beauty, success, fulfillment, peace and power will be expressed through us automatically.

All we need do is simply release the blocks that our false beliefs in separation have formed.

We cannot stop the flow of God within and around us. We can only block or cloud it. If we will simply release all thoughts, emotions, and beliefs that contradict our true God nature, we will all naturally express our own versions of freedom, love, abundance, beauty, success, fulfillment, peace and power.

The Godness within us is much like water. It flows through us naturally and it can only be deflected by the boulders of false beliefs we put in its way. All we need do to create anything is to release the blocks and allow our Godness to naturally flow through us in its divine expression. As we release the blocks, the stream turns into a river and finally an ocean washing through us. Our prayers become more like an acknowledgment of the flow of God within us and a releasing of any blocks in the way.

An example would be, "I acknowledge my oneness with God. There is no place He is that I am not. There is nothing He is that I am not. I experience this moment, being and having everything in the universe. There is nothing that isn't mine already. I release any thoughts or emotions that conflict with this and rest in the knowledge that this abundance that is already mine is being expressed through me this moment. God willed my abundance and I accept and allow it to be expressed through me and I gratefully receive its expression into my physical world."

Eventually, as our belief in our oneness with God is strengthened, there is no more need for definitions, thoughts or words. Our prayers simply become an experience of who we really are. We experience in each moment what it is like to be the God that we are.

Are there any ways to make my prayers more powerful?

All prayer is powerful because it stimulates our divine powers of creation.

***Prayer is most powerful when we know
that we are not separate from God
and we allow ourselves to focus on,
and experience, that fact.***

Sometimes we may know that we are not separate from God but we allow the busyness of life to keep us from focusing on that. Sometimes we try to stay focused but, deep inside, we really don't know that we are one with God. The powerful prayer strikes a balance of both.

***Real power comes from knowing
we are one with God and
staying focused on that.***

This allows us to take prayer out into our daily lives. Our lives can be a literal string of moments where we are continually focused on our oneness with God.

***Our prayer then becomes a powerful way
of life and our life becomes a powerful prayer.***

Prayer is self-discipline which comes as a result of discovering God's will and then making the necessary adjustments within one's thoughts, feelings, and acts.
—Charles L. Allen

For what is prayer but the expansion of yourself into the living ether?
—Kahlil Gibran

Chapter 10

The Real Miracle

*There is nothing outside you.
That is what you must ultimately learn.*
—A Course in Miracles

We continued to write on this book to catalog our experiences. As Barbara worked happily in her new job, Jimmie learned how to play the stock market by aligning his intellect and intuition. He even wrote a letter about how he was learning to trade to the software company that he used and they published his letter.

All along, both of us kept thinking that we would get an overwhelming financial avalanche from somewhere that would solve all of our problems. Instead, what we experienced were many small miracles and manifestations of our desires. In fact, we reached almost all of our financial goals.

We received checks from unexpected sources. We were given things that we needed and wanted. Some of our stocks rose even when the stock market tumbled. We received unsolicited job offers that turned out to be very loving places to work. We received more financial manifestations and miracles than we care to name.

We don't think the financial miracles that have shown up in our lives are over nor do we think they ever will be. We believe that these everyday miracles, financial and otherwise, are a natural part of living. We believe that these everyday miracles are simply a result of aligning ourselves with our Godness, trusting our Godness and then allowing the miracles to flow into physical form. But that's not the real miracle. Even if a financial avalanche were to appear, that would not be the real miracle.

The real miracle is the change that has taken place within each of us.

The real miracle is that we have let go of wanting something outside of ourselves to come and save us from anything we perceive as a problem. We know that there is nothing outside of us that can ever really save us because we don't need saving. We know that we are already sufficient for any circumstance, person or place we attract.

The real miracle is that we have let go of seeing ourselves as bodies. We know that, instead, we are a powerful energy, capable of doing, being and creating literally anything.

The real miracle is that we've stopped being victims. Even though we may not consciously understand the circumstances in our lives, we know that we created them with our past thoughts, beliefs, emotions and/or decisions. We also know that we are powerful enough to change them and create new circumstances in our lives.

The real miracle is that we know and trust the Godness within us. Even though we may not consciously understand the synchronicity at play in our lives, we trust that the Godness within us is constantly at work expressing our God energy in a perfect physical expression. All we need to do is allow the flow and remove the blocks to what God has already willed for us.

The real miracle is that we know who we really are, using God's definition as He created us to be. We know that our energy is one with God's energy and that we share in all that He is and has. We know that whatever identity we find appealing here on earth (i.e.: Gemini, successful, thin, New Agers, wealthy, kind, etc.) it can never hold a candle to our real identity. All identities we cling to here on earth are just more ways to separate ourselves from our fellow man. And as we separate ourselves from our fellow man, we separate ourselves from God. We now know that we must let go of all identity other than the one God gave to us.

The real miracle is that we have lost our fear. The challenges of being a human no longer get a response. The fear of lack no longer gets a response. The same goes for limitedness, loneliness, danger and sickness. We simply don't respond anymore.

The real miracle is that we now live authentically. What we mean by that is that we think, believe, feel and act in alignment with who we know ourselves to be. Integrity means to us the degree to which we are authentic. We are now living in integrity with ourselves.

Living these philosophies is not a perfect exercise. We all have our moments of falling back into the lie of separation and out of integrity with ourselves. But having experienced the real miracle within ourselves, we know that we can never go back to the fear and false beliefs that almost destroyed us and we know that we'll never want to.

The only desire we have left is that you find the real miracle for yourself.

Have you ever sat very quietly without any movement? You try it, sit really still, with your back straight, and observe what your mind is doing. Don't try to control it, don't say it should not jump from one thought to another, but just be aware of how your mind is jumping. Don't do anything about it, but watch it as from the banks of a river you watch the river flow by. In the flowing river there are so many things—fishes, leaves, dead animals—but it is always living, moving and your mind is like that. It is everlastingly restless, flitting from one thing to another like a butterfly . . . just watch your mind. It is great fun. If you try it as fun, as an amusing thing, you will find that the mind begins to settle down without any effort on your part to control it. There is then no censor, no judge, no evaluator; and when the mind is thus very quiet of itself, spontaneously still, you will discover what it is to be gay. Do you know what gaiety is? It is just to laugh, to take delight in anything or nothing, to know the joy of living, smiling, looking straight into the face of another without any sense of fear.

—J. Krishnamurti

Epilogue

As we applied the process of learning about the real miracle, to ourselves and our lives, we eventually saw that the culmination of what we really wanted was to live in what we called, "financial and time freedom."

On December 10, 2008 we moved to Northern California and by February we were in our gorgeous new home, perched on a mountain side overlooking a beautiful lake with no immediate neighbors around us. We were finally living in financial and time freedom. And in that milieu, in the joy and freedom of just being "us," we were able to complete what we started in 1988, at the very beginning of our relationship.

We began to trust what we had learned and eventually began living in the essence of our very being. The differences between us seemed to have vanished without us even realizing it. Our relationship had in fact become a vehicle for spiritual awakening, the intention for our relationship that we had adopted when we first got together. We had become the real miracle.

Barbara left the physical on August 31, 2010

About the Authors

Barbara and Jimmie Lewis were co-authors of two books, *The Energy of Life* and *The Real Miracle*. They wrote each book as a way of solidifying what they were learning about life and as a way of sharing what they learned with the rest of the world.

Barbara and Jimmie helped each other learn about the energy of life from the Spring of 1988 until the Spring of 2002 when they learned that miraculous living was an inside job. They went through a life-changing process that stripped away all of their worldly security and caused them to rely only on their inner being and discovered the real miracle within.

When Barbara and Jimmie got together as a couple in 1988 they knew instantly that their relationship was to be a vehicle for spiritual awakening. They went to graduate school together and became counseling psychologists with a double major in transpersonal psychology and relationships in order to learn everything they could about relationships and spiritual awakening. As licensed psychotherapists they specialized in relationships.

When Barbara and Jimmie manifested their vision of living in financial and time freedom they moved from busy lives in Houston to a mountain retreat in Northern California. Their remaining time together, and how they used their relationship for spiritual awakening, is beautifully expressed in Jimmie's moving account of their lives in his third book, *A Holy Relationship: The Memoir of One Couple's Transformation.*

For personal appearances, workshops, retreats or group sessions:
jimmie@jimmielewis.com
www.jimmielewis.com

www.ingramcontent.com/pod-product-compliance
Lightning Source LLC
Chambersburg PA
CBHW071919290426
44110CB00013B/1412